Modern English Idioms

with exercises

Linton Stone M.A., Ph.D.

Tutor in English as a Second Language
West London College

Evans Brothers Limited

Published by Evans Brothers Limited
Montague House, Russell Square
London WC1B 5BX

Evans Brothers (Nigeria Publishers) Limited
PMB 5164 Jericho Road
Ibadan

First published 1972
Third impression 1975

Printed in Great Britain by
The Garden City Press Limited
Letchworth, Hertfordshire SG6 1JS
ISBN 0 237 28950 4

PRA 4196

Contents

	page
Introduction	v
Animals (Domestic)	1
Animals (Wild)	14
Flowers	24
Trees	28
The Body	35
Clothes	47
Colours	54
Food	64
Drink	74
The Weather	80
General Exercises on all Ten Sections	91

Introduction

'The hand that rocks the cradle has kicked the bucket.' Yes, agreed; there is this danger in teaching, learning, studying, or better, absorbing idioms. But it is only a danger if the purpose of teaching is misunderstood, or if a book like this is misused. Incidentally neither of these renowned chestnuts appears in these pages. No one, of course, speaks English entirely in idioms. It is to be hoped, therefore, since this is an entire book of them, that students and teachers will not mistakenly think of it as an encouragement to use nothing but idiom.

The aims here are: a little at a time, a little and well, and an awareness of some of the high-frequency items in the huge range of English idiom. (What is there that hasn't got or given its idiom? As with Shakespeare quotations, there is one for nearly everything.) An essential part of the book is the exercises which make sure that the student is using idiom correctly, not for example using the wrong article, 'a' for 'the', nor otherwise slipping up on the tiny details that preserve idiom and give it its recognizable flavour and without which it becomes farce, custard pie and ultimately, inevitably, the heroic Hyman Kaplan with his 'funny' English (or, as it happened, American).

Plan: The plan of the book is ten sections, each on a separate subject with one to three short sets of recap questions throughout the section and a complete set of exercises at the end of each section. At the end of the book there is a large section of general exercises on the entire book.

Exercises: The exercises include direct questions on idiom as well as on language items combined with idiom. There are multiple choice and free response questions, the latter including completions and sentence writing. As an exercise, sentence writing using a given word should (may one suggest) not be ignored, this being one of the fullest of free responses, bringing out the student's ability in the patterns of his own choice.

Language items: Lexical and structural items on which questions are asked include articles, tenses, active and passive forms, phrasal verbs, prepositions, non-finites, conditionals, word order and concord. There are also questions designed to show a general awareness of correct English. And, as has been said, throughout the exercises each question is also a question on idiom.

Examples; questions: These are given as separate sentences, not passages, as the chance of idioms occurring in a string, except for humour, is rare. The separate sentence is the more natural form and typifies the occasional use of idiom.

How to use the book: For reference; in class as part of the comprehension and composition work of whatever course is being followed; for discussion and general oral and written work, and as ancillary material. Further lexical and structural work could be devised on the lines of the exercises that follow each section, and a teacher using drills and language games could profitably draw on idiom for part of his material – interrogative, negative, negative-interrogative and various other verb forms could well be practised using idioms.

Like a grain or two of preserving salt, there is the occasional proverb, though for teachers (who are never satisfied – most fortunately, since there would be something wanting in their essential critical sense if this were so) there will doubtless be omissions of this or that favourite idiom. One cannot please everyone all the time, either teacher or student, and the teacher has always the opportunity to remedy omissions.

Idiom is a part of the work of teaching and learning English, no small part because all English speakers use idiom in larger or smaller amounts. Not to know some idiom is not to know the living language. To know a lot of idiom and to use a lot of idiom is to know nothing about idiom – it is more likely than not a verbal disaster. To know a reasonable amount of idiom and to use it sparingly is to have a true insight into a living language. This is the true wisdom of idiom and the ultimate aim of this book.

Animals (Domestic)

bull
(n.) take the bull by the horns = face and try to deal with a difficulty or problem instead of avoiding it
The government took the bull by the horns and asked the public to report any new price rises.

bulldoze
(v.) bully or force someone into doing something

bullnecked
(adj.) man with a very thick neck

calf-love
(n.) young boy's or girl's love

cat
(n.) 1. spiteful woman

(adj. of this) catty

(n.) 2. let the cat out of the bag = reveal a secret accidentally
He let the cat out of the bag when he told her he was coming to her birthday party. She didn't know they were giving her a party.

(n.) 3. not room to swing a cat in = very narrow space
There isn't room to swing a cat in this office.

(n.) 4. When the cat's away the mice will play. Often used as 'When the cat's away . . .' = People get up to mischief when there's no one to watch over them.

(adj.) 1. cat-and-dog life = life/relationship full of quarrels
That family leads a cat-and-dog life.

(adj.) 2. cat and mouse game = cruel/unkind domination of weaker person by stronger one; often toying with or torturing s'o[1]
The captain always finds some new excuse for not

---
[1] s'o=someone   s't=something

1

giving the soldiers leave. It's a cat and mouse game.

(n.) It's raining cats and dogs = It's raining very heavily.

see **fox**, Animals (Wild), p.15

cat-burglar   (n.) burglar who enters a building by climbing up its side

catcall   (n. and v.) sharp whistle of disapproval from audience or crowd (as at the theatre or a meeting)

cat-nap   (n.) short sleep in a chair (not in bed)
I sat in the armchair and had a cat-nap for twenty minutes.

see **kitten**, p.6

cow   (v.) frighten s'o into doing or accepting s't; or intimidate s'o
She cowed them with one look.

(adj. of this) cowed
They had a very cowed manner.

dog   (n.) 1. a gay/lucky/old/sly dog = a lively/lucky/roguish/sly person (used affectionately)
Harry's a sly dog. He didn't say he'd won £2,000.

(n.) 2. go to the dogs = ruin oneself/be ruined/deteriorate morally
Jack's gone to the dogs altogether. He drinks all day long now.

(n.) 3. have/lead a dog's life = have an unhappy life; often simply, 'It's a dog's life.'

(n.) 4. lead s'o a dog's life = constantly make s'o unhappy
He leads her a dog's life.

(n.) 5. give a dog a bad name (and hang him) = give s'o a bad reputation and it often remains; often used simply as 'Give a dog a bad name'
'No one trusts him since that woman called him a thief.'
'Yes, it's unfair, but give a dog a bad name. . . .'

(n.) 6. help a lame dog over a stile = help s'o in

trouble; often used without 'over a stile'
'I don't mind helping a lame dog now and again, but I'm not made of money (= rich).'

(n.) 7. let sleeping dogs lie = avoid s'o or a situation or topic that could cause trouble or could revive an old trouble
'Don't mention George's name to Roger. They had a very bad row two years ago. Let sleeping dogs lie, if you follow me.'

(n.) 8. underdog = s'o who has to do what others tell him
Pity the underdog. He seems to have no life of his own. Arthur will always be an underdog. He's afraid to give orders.

(n.) 9. put on some dog = give oneself an air of importance
'You'd better put on some dog if you want them to consider you for the job as manager!'

(n.) 10. You can't/It's hard to/teach an old dog new tricks = It's difficult to teach new ways to s'o set in his habits.

(n.) 11. a dog in the manger = s'o who stops others enjoying/using s't that is useless to himself

(v.) dog s'o = follow behind s'o closely (like a detective)
(adj.) dogged [dɔgid] = determined

dogsbody
(n.) s'o who is like a slave because everyone gives him orders; often with 'general'.
He's the general dogsbody in the office.

dog-tired
(adj.) tired out/exhausted
I'm dog-tired after that walk.

donkey
(n.) foolish person

(adj.) 1. do the donkey work = do the hard/heavy work of a job; often monotonous, routine work
'It's easy enough to read a lot of statistics but who does the donkey work and prepares them?'

(adj.) 2. I haven't seen him for donkey's ages/years = for a long time.

3

mule	(n.) stubborn person
	He's/a mule/as stubborn as a mule.
	(adj. of this) mulish (n. –ness, adv. –ly)

goat	(n.) 1. separate the sheep from the goats = separate the good from the wicked, or decide which are which (Matthew 25, 33)
	It didn't take the new teacher long to separate the sheep from the goats.
	(n.) 2. It/That gets my goat = It/That annoys me.
	(n.) 3. play the (giddy) goat = play the fool
	(n.) scapegoat = s'o blamed/punished for another's mistakes/wrongs
	They made a colonel the scapegoat for the general's mistake.

Short questions

1. To let the cat out of the bag means
   A to give a party   B to cause trouble   C to give away a secret
   D to talk about one's troubles
2. Leading a dog's life means being
   A unhappy   B happy   C busy   D tired
3. The really hard work is the . . .
   A goat   B horse   C mule   D donkey/work
4. Stop fooling = Stop playing the
   A horse   B mule   C goat   D donkey
5. What does 'bull-necked' mean?
6. Use 'cat' in an idiom.

---

horse	(n.) 1. a dark horse = s'o whose abilities/chances are unknown
	Peter will pass the exam but Edward's a dark horse.
	(n.) 2. flog a dead horse = waste time/energy on s't already established/decided/finished/settled; try to revive interest in s't already past.
	'You're flogging a dead horse if you're trying to make him change his political views.'
	Trying to interest the general public in fourteenth century music is like flogging a dead horse.

4

(n.) 3. look a gift horse in the mouth = find fault with a present (from telling a horse's age by its teeth) 'He only gave me a cheap bicycle.' 'I daresay, but you shouldn't look a gift horse in the mouth.'

(n.) 4. be on/get up on/one's high horse = behave as though one is superior
He got up on his high horse because he's related to the Prime Minister.

(n.) 5. That's a horse of another/a different/colour = That's another/a different/matter.
'Taking the exam is one thing but passing it is a horse of a different colour.'

(n.) 6. Michael eats/works like a horse = a lot/hard

(n.) 7. put the cart before the horse = do things in the wrong order
Learn to walk before you run. Don't try putting the cart before the horse.

(n.) 8. You've backed the wrong horse = You've made the wrong/a bad/decision.

(n.) 9. Hold your horses! = Wait a moment!/Don't be in such a hurry.

(n.) 10. Wild horses won't/wouldn't/couldn't drag/draw it (the truth/a secret) from/out of me.

(adj.) (straight) from the horse's mouth = a reliable tip, piece of advice or information
It's/I've had it/I've got it/ straight from the horse's mouth. The new hotel isn't making any money.

horsy	(adj.) 1. (person) associated with horses, horse-racing
	(adj.) 2. bossy and loud-voiced; often used of woman She's very horsy.
horseplay	(n.) noisy, rough play, usually in fun; e.g. a pillow fight, or snatching a friend's hat and throwing it from one to the other He had to stop their horseplay when it got too rough.
horse-sense	(n.) good/common/sense
hound	(v.) chase/worry s'o

The soldiers hounded the deserters all over the country.
The landlord hounded the tenants until they paid their rent.
He was hounded out of the country by public anger.

kitten   (n.) have kittens = be very surprised/annoyed/frightened; often with 'nearly'
She nearly had kittens when he dropped her teapot.

lamb   (n.) Heaven tempers the wind to the shorn lamb = Heaven protects the weak/unprotected (makes the wind blow less coldly on the freshly sheared lambs).

see **sheep** below

pig   (n.) 1. dirty/greedy/bad-mannered person

(n.) 2. buy a pig in a poke = buy s't on chance (not examining/seeing it/knowing its value); from Fr. *poche*, Engl. bag or sack
You often buy a pig in a poke when you buy by letter.

(n.) 3. make a pig of oneself = be greedy/eat too much/overeat

(v.) pig it = live in a dirty uncomfortable way

(adj.) piggy = greedy

(adj.) piggish = dirty/greedy

pigsty   (n.) any place that is/looks dirty

pig-headed   (adj.) stubborn

(n. of this) pig-headedness

puppy fat   (adj.) the fat that girls often have before adolescence

sheep   (n.) 1. stupid/timid person(s)

(n.) 2. the black sheep of the family = disreputable member of a family

(n.) 3. (might) as well be hanged for a sheep as (for) a lamb = One might as well commit a big crime/sin if the punishment is the same as for a small one.

(adj.) cast/make sheep's eyes at s'o = look at s'o in a

foolish, amorous way (like a sheep looking sideways)

sheepish   (adj.) awkward/self-conscious/timid

(adv. of this) sheepishly

see **goat,** p. 4; **wolf,** p. 18

Short questions

1. To hound someone is to . . . him.
   A worry   B help   C phone   D attack
2. If you buy a pig in a poke you . . . what you are getting.
   A know   B don't know   C can see   D don't pay for
3. To be very surprised = to have
   A goats   B cats   C mules   D kittens
4. What sort of a horse is a person whose abilities are unknown?
   A light   B grey   C dark   D black
5. Explain 'He behaved very sheepishly'.
6. Write a sentence using 'puppy' as an idiom.

Verbs and Other Forms

bark   1. speak in a commanding/sharp voice
'Do as you're told,' he barked.

2. You're barking up the wrong tree = You're making a mistake (complaining to the wrong person/assuming the wrong thing).
'If you think she did it, you're barking up the wrong tree.'

(n.) 1. cough, or sound of gunfire
Nick's got an awful cough. You can hear his bark everywhere.
There was a constant bark of guns. (and verb form)

(n.) 2. His bark is worse than his bite = When he's angry/bad-tempered he says he'll do violent things but he never does.

bellow   roar (q.v.)/make a loud, deep noise
He bellowed at them to keep quiet.
They bellowed with rage/pain.

bleat
say s't/speak/weakly
He bleated that he was unwell.

(n.) a bleat of despair

bray
verb for noise made by donkey; used abusively
The politicians were braying (about) how much they had achieved.
He was braying about his own achievements.

grunt
make a noise showing annoyance/boredom/irritation/tiredness
He grunted in an annoyed way when she asked him where he had been.
She grunted an answer.

(n.) He gave a grunt of irritation and walked out.

harness
control in order to use
Why don't they harness that river and produce electricity?

(n.) 1. in harness = doing one's regular job
He'll be back in harness on Monday.
Old Hamilton died in harness.

(n.) 2. (run/work) in double harness = work with a partner

prance
1. walk about in a self-important way
'Who does she think she is, prancing in here/about/as if she owned the place?'

2. dance/jump happily
They were prancing/at the news/with joy.

rub
rub s'o up the wrong way (like stroking a cat the wrong way) = annoy/irritate s'o

scratch
(n.) up to scratch = fit/up to the required standard
His health/work/isn't up to scratch.

trot
1. humorous synonym for walk in the sense of go/leave
'It's getting late. I must be trotting along.'

(n.) of this = a walk
'Let's go for a (short) trot.'

8

(n.) at a steady trot = at a regular, satisfactory rate (walk/work)
The class is going at a steady trot.

2. show one's knowledge; produce/quote/say in support
When we talked about peace he trotted out all the old arguments for nuclear weapons.

wag/waggle 1. finger movement to show disapproval
She wagged her finger as she told him off.

2. talk scandal; usually used with 'tongue'
Tongues were wagging over the divorce.

wallow enjoy sensual pleasures or behave over-emotionally: in alcohol/luxury/self-pity/sentimentality; often with 'in'
She was very sorry for herself; she was wallowing in self-pity.

Short questions

1. If you rub a person up the wrong way, he is
   A annoyed   B pleased   C puzzled   D bored
2. A person who does a regular job is
   A on the trot   B in harness   C bleating away   D on the bark
3. They were prancing because they were
   A tired   B unhappy   C happy   D hungry
4. She . . . her finger at him very angrily.
   A wallowed   B brayed   C bellowed   D wagged
5. Ada's father grunted at her. Why might this have been?
6. Give an idiomatic use of 'bark'.

Details

bit (n.) take the bit between one's teeth = get out of control
When Henry won the pools he took the bit between his teeth and went completely mad for a while.

blinkers (n.) go round with blinkers on = be unable/refuse/to see the realities of life

(adj. of this) blinkered

fur   (n.) make the fur fly = cause trouble (*see* **fox,** p. 15 no. 3)

nosebag   (n.) put the nosebag(s) on = eat
'It's one o'clock. Time to put the nosebags on.'

paw   (n.) hand

(v.) touch/handle s't awkwardly/s'o against their will
He pawed all the books on the shelf.
'Stop pawing those cakes and take one!'
She told him to stop pawing her.

reins   (n.) 1. hold the reins = be in charge/control
Movo Petrol is a huge company. I wonder who really holds the reins.

(n.) 2. keep a tight rein on = control firmly/give little freedom to

(v.) rein (s'o) in = control oneself/s'o

saddle   (v.) saddle s'o with s't = put a big responsibility on s'o
He found himself saddled with his widowed sister and all her children.

spur   (n.) on the spur of the moment = impulsively/suddenly

(v.) encourage; often with 'on'
Success spurred her (on) to work even harder in life.

tail   (n.) 1. on s'o's tail = following s'o/intending to reprimand s'o
He'll be on your tail when he finds all your mistakes.

(n.) 2. turn tail = run away

(n.) 3. He went home with his tail between his legs = He went home defeated/depressed by s't.

(n.) 4. in plural, tails = man's long black jacket for evening wear
Older men prefer tails to dinner jackets.

(n.) 5. in plural, 'Heads or tails?' = the choice of one or other side of a coin when it is spun (tossed in the air) to decide s't by chance

(v.) 1. tail after s'o = follow s'o

10

(v.) 2. tail s'o = follow/shadow/s'o (as a detective does)

(v) 3. tail away/off = end unsatisfactorily; fall behind/get smaller
The story tailed off very dully.
The line of trees tailed away/off into the distance.
Some of the soldiers began tailing away.

whisker (n.) tiny distance
Could you move that ornament just a whisker?

wool (adj.) dyed-in-the-wool = absolute/convinced/out-and-out/thorough-going
He's a dyed-in-the-wool traditionalist.

(n.) He tried to pull the wool over my eyes = He tried to deceive/fool me.

woolgathering (adj.) absent-minded/day-dreaming

(n. of this) woolgatherer
He's a bit of a woolgatherer.

woolly (adj.) confused/unclear/in argument or thought
He's/His ideas are/very woolly.

(n. of this) woolliness

Exercises

A. Give or say the correct answer: A, B, C or D.

1. He's a general dogsbody. This means he
   A is an army leader   B gives orders   C takes orders   D is a mongrel dog
2. Being frightened into obeying someone is the same as being
   A dogged   B bullnecked   C catcalled   D cowed
3. Which animal is used in the idiom meaning a person with a bad reputation in a family?
   A horse   B bull   C sheep   D pig
   What is the idiom?
4. Wasting time on a question that has been settled is
   A taking the bull by the horns   B letting the cat out of the bag
   C going to the dogs   D flogging a dead horse

5. Greedy = A catty B piggy C horsy D dogged
6. Impulsively = on the . . . of the moment
   A spur B harness C reins D saddle
7. Time for lunch = Time to put on the
   A saddle B blinkers C nosebag D whiskers
8. Someone who is day-dreaming is
   A an underdog B doing the donkey work C playing the goat
   D woolgathering
9. He was showing off by telling people all he had done.
   He was . . . about what he had done.
   A bellowing B bleating C barking D braying
10. Straight from the horse's mouth = A very quickly
    B unreliable C large teeth D a good tip

B. Complete the sentences using a suitable idiomatic verb and verb form.

1. I wish she'd stop . . . about in that self-important way.
2. We could hardly hear him when he . . . that he felt sick.
3. When I reached my front door, there was Johnson right behind me.
   He must . . . me all the way home.
4. They . . . it in a very uncomfortable flat for about three months.
5. He always . . . at the staff like a sergeant-major.
   I've asked him not to do it.
6. They could hear Jones . . . out the same theories about the earth
   being flat.
7. The story . . . away very unexcitingly.
8. It was too much for Patrick winning all that money last year. For a
   time he . . . completely to the dogs.
9. The burglar took everything he could find in the flat.
   Might as well be . . . for a sheep as a lamb, he thought.
10. If Peter . . . all his ideas he could produce something great.

C. Write down, or say, sentences using each of the following as, or in, an
   idiom.

1. pig-headed 2. sly dog 3. puppy fat 4. sheep's eyes 5. fur
6. saddle 7. scapegoat 8. high horse 9. mulish 10. donkey's years

D. Rearrange each of these word groups correctly to form sentences.

1. led dog a and life cat they
2. him house bulldozed into she a buying
3. play away mice will the when cat's the
4. known Jack's sheep the family as black of the
5. better your you'd stop horseplay
6. round blinkers goes he on with

7. wool eyes tried they over the pull to my
8. to she him asked not her paw
9. James legs had between tail his his
10. John bit his teeth between the took

E. Find the numbered sentences which match the lettered ones.

1. He was dog-tired.
2. He's wearing his tails.
3. It was a case of calf-love.
4. That is something else altogether.
5. He just won't do what you ask him.
6. You won't change his opinions.
7. Freddie was saddled with his family.
8. What a filthy place it was!
9. Heaven tempers the wind and so forth, they say.
10. They keep a tight rein on Willy.

  a He had to support his two brothers.
  b It's a horse of a different colour.
  c Jack's a dyed-in-the-wool vegetarian.
  d Patrick's very mulish.
  e John survived even though he lost his money.
  f It was just like a pigsty.
  g Juliet married very young.
  h Michael was exhausted.
  i He can't do what he wants.
  j John is in evening dress.

Animals (Wild)

ape (v.) copy the behaviour of
The child aped/was aping his parents.

badger (v.) annoy with questions or requests
She badgered her husband until he bought her the coat.
She kept badgering him with questions about (the price of) his furniture.

bear (n.) like a bear with a sore head = angry
He had lost his train and was like a bear with a sore head.

(*Note.* The white bear at the North Pole is called a polar bear.)

buck (n.) male deer or rabbit; perhaps the origin of 'pass the buck' = avoid blame or responsibility
No one will take the blame for the mistake. They keep passing the buck.

bunny *see* **rabbit**, p. 18

crocodile (n.) group of schoolgirls walking two by two; often with 'in'
About thirty girls from the local school were going along the road in a noisy crocodile.

(adj.) crocodile tears = sorrow which is not genuine
She wept (from 'weep') a few crocodile tears at her stepmother's funeral.
'She was very sorry to hear the news,'
her father said.
'Crocodile tears,' replied her aunt.

cub (n.) 1. badly-behaved young man (often with 'young')

'That young cub had better behave himself or he'll get into trouble!'
'Cheeky young cubs!' the elderly man called after a group of youths who had pushed him off the pavement.

(n.) 2. junior Boy Scout

elephant

(n.) 1. a white elephant = gift, possession or idea that causes its owner a lot of trouble or expense, and is therefore useless
That car John won is a white elephant. He just can't afford to run it.

(n.) 2. memory like an elephant
Michael never forgets anything. He has a memory like an elephant.

elephantine

(adj.) large/heavy/clumsy
An elephantine young woman took up the whole seat on the bus.
A large, awkward man, he walked with elephantine movements.

ferret

(n.) eyes like a ferret = vicious/cruel-looking eyes

(v.) find by searching/researching/investigating (rather like a detective)
The insurance company ferreted out the truth about the fire.

fox

(n.) 1. as crafty/cunning/sly as a fox
Be careful of Jack. He's as crafty as a fox.

(n.) 2. crafty/cunning/sly/untrustworthy person; often with 'old'
Be careful of Jack. He's an old fox.

(n.) 3. put the fox among the geese = to make trouble (also = 'put the cat among the pigeons')
'Mr Allen said he was sure some of the staff were stealing.'
'I bet that put the fox among the geese.' 'It certainly did.'

foxy

(adj.) crafty/cunning/sly/untrustworthy
He's too foxy for my liking.

| **frog** | (n.) have a frog in one's throat = have phlegm at the back of one's throat, making it difficult to speak |
| | I've got a frog in my throat. Excuse me while I cough. Ah, that's better. |

| **frogman** | (n.) swimmer who uses underwater equipment; usually member of a naval service of frogmen |

| **frogmarch** | (v.) carry away a person (usually a prisoner) by force face downwards; four people hold each a leg or an arm |
| | The prisoner refused to leave the court and had to be frogmarched to the police van. |

hare	(n.) 1. mad as a March hare = wild/stupid/mad in behaviour
	George is a very reckless driver. He's as mad as a March hare.
	(n.) 2. run with the hare and hunt with the hounds = try to be on good terms with both sides in a disagreement (often slyly rather than openly)
	'He tells the management one thing and the men another.'
	'Yes, he runs with the hare and hunts with the hounds, I'm afraid.'
	(n.) 3. hare and hounds = a paper chase. A game where a small group leave a trail of torn-up pieces of paper for a larger group to follow.
	(v.) hare away/off = run away/off very quickly
	He hared off the moment I shouted 'Stop!'.

| **hare-brained** | (adj.) rash/foolish/irresponsible |
| | That was a hare-brained thing to do, leaving the car unlocked all night. |

| **hare-lip** | (n.) division in the upper lip |
| | His appearance was somewhat spoilt by a hare-lip. |

Short questions

1. A double line of schoolgirls =
   A an ape B a fox C a crocodile D a snake

2. 'Like a bear with a sore head' =
   A stupid B angry C excited D ill
3. He was frogmarched away = He was
   A helped B led C carried D wheeled
4. Crocodile tears are A false B large C not salty D coffee sugar
5. What does 'passing the buck' mean?
6. Write a sentence using 'fox' as an idiom.

---

hog

(n.) 1. greedy person; often used with greedy
He's a greedy hog.

(n.) 2. road hog = driver who takes too much of the road

(n.) 3. go the whole hog = do something fully/completely
'If you're prepared to buy an expensive car you may as well go the whole hog and buy a Rolls.'

(v.) eat greedily
There were only six potatoes and he hogged the lot.

leopard

(n.) The leopard doesn't/can't change its spots = A person doesn't/can't change his character.

lion

(n.) the lion's share = the larger or largest part
John took the lion's share of the family money.

lion-hearted

(adj.) brave

lionize

(v.) treat as a celebrity, often by inviting to social gatherings
The author was lionized by numerous literary groups.

mole-hill

(n.) make a mountain out of a mole-hill = make a small difficulty/problem seem like a large one

monkey

(n.) mischievous/playful person (often a child)
He's a (cheeky) little monkey.

(adj.) monkey business = suspicious behaviour; cheating
Some sort of monkey business goes on in that shop over change. It's often short.

(v.) monkey with s't = interfere/play about/with s't
'Don't monkey with my watch!'

17

mouse	(n.) nervous/shy/timid person
	(adj. of this) mousy
rabbit	(n.) a bunny or bunny rabbit = a child's word for rabbit
	(n.) a Bunny = a club hostess with a costume in some ways like a rabbit
	(adj. of this) Bunny Club. She works at the Bunny Club in Park Lane.
	(v.) go rabbitting = go hunting for rabbits
rat	(n.) 1. one who deserts friends or a cause; often used with dirty and little 'He's a dirty little rat,' she said. 'He's working for the enemy.'
	(n.) 2. smell a rat = be suspicious of a person/situation 'I smell a rat. I don't think he's telling the truth.'
rat-race	(n.) the rat-race = the general struggle that takes place to survive The rat-race is at its worst in the big towns.
ratty	(adj.) irritable What's wrong with Michael today? He's very ratty.
rhinoceros	(n.) He's got a hide like a rhinoceros = He's very thick-skinned/insensitive.
snake	(n.) treacherous person pretending to be a friend
	(adj. of this) snaky
turtle	turn turtle = of ships, turn over/capsize
whale	(n.) have a whale of a time = have a wonderful time
wolf	(n.) 1. a wolf in sheep's clothing = snake (n.) above
	(n.) 2. keep the wolf from the door = earn enough to keep oneself (and one's family)
	(v.) eat greedily; often with 'down' He wolfed (down) his dinner.

zebra   (adj.) a zebra crossing = street-crossing with black and white stripes, for walkers

---

Short questions

1. To turn turtle = A to faint   B to go mad   C to turn over   D to swim
2. A road hog = A a pedestrian   B a cyclist   C a quick driver   D a greedy driver
3. A snaky person is someone you
   A distrust   B can't catch   C trust   D think is too thin
4. If you took the lion's share you would
   A be stealing   B have the biggest amount   C have the smallest amount   D be trying to annoy someone
5. Explain 'We were having a whale of a time'.
6. Use 'rhinoceros' in an idiom.

Verbs and Other Forms

burrow   (v.) search by looking under or digging into a collection of items
She burrowed under a pile of books to find the letter.

breed   cause/bring about
Fear often breeds hate.
Familiarity breeds contempt.

(adj.) well-bred = taught to behave well;
a well-bred person

(n.) a person of good breeding

growl   speak angrily/threateningly
'What's the matter now?' he growled.

hiss   (v.) 1. noise of disapproval, often at a public performance
The audience hissed the actors off the stage.

(v.) 2. noise of steam
Steam was hissing from the kettle.

howl   (v.) 1. cry with pain

The child was howling with toothache.

(v.) 2. make sounds of amusement or contempt
They howled with laughter/scorn.

hunt for look/search for (place of a hidden object is not
known)
She's been hunting everywhere for her missing ring.

hunt out look/search for by selection (in known place)
The librarian asked his assistant to hunt out Volumes
three and seven of the encyclopedia for him.

hunt down search for and find (often a prisoner or criminal)
The wanted man was hunted down in a wood.

matey (adj. from mate) friendly, sociable (often + 'with')
The new neighbours were very matey.
He's very matey with the manager.

prowl walk about carefully, looking for a chance to steal
At one o'clock she noticed two men in the street who
looked as though they were prowling (about).

(n.) on the prowl = prowling
The men looked as though they were on the prowl.

prowler (n. of the person)

purr express or show pleasure at something
'It's a beautiful present,' she purred.

roar shout angrily/with laughter/with pain
'Get out of my way,' he roared at them.

(n.) a sound of anger/laughter
He gave a roar of anger/laughter.

snarl speak angrily/unpleasantly
'It's all your fault,' he snarled.

Parts

claw (n.) in plural = hands of greedy person

His relatives were all waiting to get their claws on his money.

(v.) handle greedily/viciously (often with 'at')
The women at the sale were clawing at the jumpers and blouses. Two women got so angry they began clawing at each other.

hide (n.) 1. a thick hide/hide like a rhinoceros = insensitive/ thick-skinned person
He ignored their criticisms. He had a hide like a rhinoceros.

(n.) 2. save one's hide = save oneself from justice/ punishment

see **bacon**, Food, p. 64

hiding (n.) give someone a good hiding = beat/thrash someone
The boys were given a good hiding for their rudeness.

hidebound (adj.) narrow-minded/too conventional
'You'll never change their ideas. They're far too hidebound.'

hoof (v.) walk (often with 'it')
They missed the last bus and had to hoof it.

horn (n.) 1. draw in one's horns = manage with/spend less than one had hoped
He had hoped to buy a new car. Instead he had to draw in his horns and buy another second-hand one.

(n.) 2. on the horns of a dilemma = in a difficulty, the only solutions to which are unpleasant
He was on the horns of a dilemma. He didn't know whether to pay the blackmailer (*see* **Colours** p. 55), or go to the police and risk being imprisoned.

skin, tooth, etc. *see* **The Body,** p. 42–3

shell (n.) go into/come out of one's shell = become/stop being shy

shell out (v.) pay unwillingly
I had to shell out £30 for new tyres the other day.

Exercises

A Write or say the correct answer: A, B, C or D.

1. Someone who runs away very quickly
   A apes off   B lions off   C hares off   D rabbits off
2. A present that causes its owner a lot of expense is a
   A blue fox   B polar bear   C white elephant   D frog in the throat
3. 'To make trouble' can be said idiomatically using
   A hare, hounds   B hoof, claw   C fox, geese   D purr, roar
   What is the idiom?
4. Speaking unpleasantly to someone is
   A howling   B growling   C prowling   D clawing
5. To have to economize when buying something is to
   A draw in your horns   B have a hide like a rhinoceros
   C ape someone   D pass the buck

Say the following idiomatically as far as possible.

6. He had a difficult problem. Neither of its solutions was pleasant.
7. They got hold of her money by a trick.
8. He looked in the linen basket for the missing sock.
9. The public made unpleasant sounds at the musicians.
10. The bag-snatcher followed the two women along the High Street.

B

1. The women were clawing each other means they . . . each other
   A helped   B attacked   C liked   D looked at
2. He was frogmarched away by soldiers means he
   A was taken away by force   B walked quietly   C was made to run
   D was forced to jump
3. They hoofed it all the way there means they
   A ran   B laughed   C walked   D argued
4. A memory like an elephant means a . . . memory
   A good   B bad   C lazy   D stupid
5. To be matey means to be
   A unkind   B unfriendly   C friendly   D fat

Explain these sentences.

6. They thought him well-bred.
7. The two men were obviously on the prowl.
8. He gave them a hiding.
9. Her sorrow was all crocodile tears.
10. 'Stop badgering me,' she told him.

C Rewrite, or say, these sentences replacing the part(s) in italics with an idiom.

1. She *kept on bothering* him until he bought a new car.
2. 'What are you doing that for?' he *said angrily*.
3. The new author was *invited out* by the art patrons of New York.
4. She had never known anyone so *brave*.
5. I'll meet you at that *black-and-white striped street* crossing.
6. He was looked upon as a complete *deserter*.
7. He thought her rather *a timid person*.
8. 'Don't always be so *irritable*!'
9. The whole family had gone *to shoot rabbits*.
10. They *gave great shouts of* laughter.

D Explain by writing or speaking the meaning of

1. She purred when he told her she was pretty.
2. John has a memory like an elephant.
3. She works as a Bunny.
4. He went the whole hog and bought two new suits.
5. Stop making mountains out of molehills!
6. He's got a hide like a rhinoceros.
7. 'She's hogged all the apples!'
8. 'Haven't you hunted out that stamp for me yet?'
9. He snarled the answer at the judge.
10. That was a hare-brained decision.

Flowers

daisy

(n.) 1. girl's name in English

(n.) 2. be under/pushing up/the daisies = be dead

(n.) 3. daisy-chain = necklace of linked daisies, often made by children

(n.) 4. in the simile: as fresh as a daisy = very fresh

lily

(n.) 1. girl's name in English

(adj.) 1. lily-livered = cowardly

primrose

(adj.) the primrose path = the search for/way of/idle (unthinking) pleasure
When Harry was young he followed the primrose path a little too often. Now, of course, he regrets it.

rose

(n.) 1. an English rose = a beautiful English girl
And negatively, 'She's no rose'.

(n.) 2. a bed of roses = an easy, luxurious life
Life's been a bed of roses for Ronald since he came into his uncle's money. (*see* rosy, p. 25)

(n.) 3. s't is not all roses = It has its difficulties/ disadvantages/problems.
Life's/The job's not all roses, however good it sometimes is.

(n.) 4. No rose without a thorn = Everything has its disadvantages. (*see* **thorn,** p. 26)

(n.) 5. roses in the cheeks = reddish cheeks as a sign of good health
'You need a day in the country to get the/some roses back in your cheeks.'

(n.) 6. rose window = wheel-shaped church window

(n.) 7. *sub rosa* = Latin for under the rose = under a vow of secrecy
He told her about the plan *sub rosa*.

(adj.) 1. look at/see life through rose-coloured spectacles = see only the pleasant side of life, ignoring the unpleasant side
He told her to stop looking at life through rose-coloured spectacles and become aware of some of its realities.

(adj.) 2. rose-red = red as a rose

(adj.) 3. Everything's/Life's rosy at the moment = The future looks/Prospects look/The outlook's/good.

wallflower (n.) girl at a dance who gets few offers to dance; also applied to a girl without boy-friends
She's a bit of a wallflower.

Verbs and Other Forms

droop 1. Her/His spirits drooped = She/He felt sad.

2. become tired/weak
By nine o'clock he always begins to droop.

(adj.) droopy = slow of mind/stupid

fade 1. lose beauty
She'd faded since I last saw her.

(adj. of this) She looked very faded; the good looks had all gone.
Another faded beauty. (also: Her beauty had faded.)

2. lose strength (often with 'away')
He's so ill/thin he's just fading away.
He's fading fast.

3. go gradually from memory/sight/hearing
His grandmother's early memories of London have faded.
They stood waving good-bye until the car faded from view.
The roar of traffic faded as they left London behind.

4. film/radio technique of gradually blacking out/ silencing one scene, and then bringing to light/life the next; sometimes used as 'fade in', 'fade out'

(n.) of this is often used with slow: a slow fade

plant

1. put an idea in s'o's mind
It was Lionel who planted the idea in Bernard's mind that Marjorie was unfriendly.

2. take up a position
Roy planted himself outside the front door and refused to move.

3. place on s'o or in his home/office, etc. s't that will make him seem guilty
Bennet didn't steal the diamonds. Someone planted them in his garage.

sow

1. sow the seeds of = cause the beginning of
Those meetings in small cellars sowed the seeds of the revolution. (also, be the germ of).

2. sow one's wild oats = do the usual foolish things one does in youth

3. As you sow, so shall you reap = You will be treated according to the way you behave/live.

weed

1. get rid of the less reliable/useful/valuable etc.
The teacher weeded out all the students who weren't working hard and sent them to another class.

(n.) 1. thin, weak-looking person

(adj. of this) weedy

(n.) 2. Have a weed? = Have a cigarette?

(n.) 3. widow's weeds = widow's black mourning clothes

Details

thorn

(n.) He's/She's/It's a thorn in my flesh/side = a continual annoyance one has to put up with
Alice's mother is a thorn in Bill's side. She probably sees him the same way – the usual in-law problem.

(adj.) a thorny problem/situation = a difficult/trouble-some problem (also one that causes argument)

see **Trees** (next section) for leaf, root, etc.

flowery   (adj.) flowery language = language full of ornament (fine words, figures of speech)

Short questions

1. If she isn't pretty she's no
   A lily   B daisy   C primrose   D rose
2. A wallflower is   A very popular   B not very popular
   C ambitious   D none of these
3. If the evidence was planted, it was
   A thrown away   B forgotten   C hidden   D not needed
4. . . . wild oats refers to one's young days.
   A weeding   B planting   C drooping   D sowing
5. What is poor Jim pushing up if he is dead?
6. Use 'rose' in an idiom. Explain the idiom.

Trees

birch　　　　　(v.) punish by beating with birch twigs tied together

(n. of above) instrument made in this way

chestnut　　　　(n.) very old joke (often used with 'crack')
He cracked/told some/a few/chestnuts.

nut　　　　　　(n.) 1. a hard nut = obstinate/unyielding person

(n.) 2. a hard nut to crack = a difficult problem to solve

(adj. of this) nutty (but *see below*)

(n.) 3. tough nut = rough/tough person

(n.) 4. off one's nut/be nuts = be insane/mad

(adj. of this) nutty
He's/off his nut/nuts/nutty.

nutshell　　　　(n.) in a nutshell = explained/said in very few words
(often with 'To put it . . .')
(To put it) in a nutshell, James didn't get the job.

oak　　　　　　The Oaks = a horse race run at Epsom, near London,
for three-year-old fillies (female foals)

olive　　　　　(n.) hold out the olive-branch = show that one is
ready to make peace in a dispute (quarrel/war)

willow　　　　　(adj.) a willowy young man/woman = a tall, flexible
and slender/slim young m./w.

Verbs, Other Forms and Details

blossom　　　　blossom into/out as = develop very satisfactorily

28

She's blossomed into a fine young woman.
Don's blossomed out as an artist.

branch off   1. divide into branches (railway lines/roads)
The line branches (off) just outside Windsor (also branch away).

(adj. of this) a branch line

2. branch out = expand/extend one's activities in new ways
The Universal Employment Agency has begun branching out in a big way. They now find jobs for domestic and hotel staff as well as office staff.

3. branch out on one's own = break away from a firm/group to start on one's own

(n.) Our roots are in our branches. (Bank advertisement).

bud   (n.) nip in the bud = end s't in its early stages
Bob was going to invite Peggy home but his mother soon nipped that (idea) in the bud.

(adj.) budding = beginning to develop/showing promise
A budding scientist.

bush   (n.) 1. A bird in the hand (is worth two in the bush) = An offer now is better than any number of possible ones later.

(n.) 2. to beat about the bush = discuss a subject in a way that avoids saying what has/ought to be said.
Whenever Janet asks the boss for more money he keeps beating about the bush.

bushy   (adj.) heavy/thick growth = bushy eyebrows/tail

cut   cut down = kill, usually in war or through an epidemic
(also often found with words showing an early or good stage of life)
Typhoid cut them down in their thousands.
The cavalry were cut down by the heavy guns.
He was cut down in youth/early manhood/the prime of life.

Short questions

1. Briefly = A on a chestnut   B in the branches
   C in a nutshell   D cut out
2. The plan was nipped in the bud = The plan was
   A too complicated   B too economical
   C successful   D unsuccessful
3. To crack chestnuts you have to
   A talk   B walk   C jump   D run
4. A tall, slender person is
   A oaken   B budding   C nutty   D willowy
5. 'She branched out on her own' means . . . ?
6. Use 'budding' in an idiom, and explain the idiom.

---

graft   transplant pieces of bone/skin from one person (or part of body) to another surgically

noun of this, 1. a (bone/skin) graft

(n.) 2. corrupt practices in business/politics
The critics were saying that the whole system was founded on graft.

hedge   (v.) 1. hedge s'o in/round = restrict s'o with regulations/rules

(v.) 2. hedge = avoid giving a direct/straight answer; answer evasively
'The minister hedged throughout the interview – not one direct answer to anything.'

(n.) They looked as though they'd been dragged through a hedge backwards. A simile meaning: They looked very untidy.

leaf   leaf through a book = look quickly through a book (past tense = leafed)

(n.) 1. take a leaf out of s'o's book = take s'o as an example worth copying
'Why don't you take a leaf out of John's book and study hard?'

(n.) 2. turn over a new leaf = make a new and better start; reform

'Why don't you turn over a new leaf and do your homework regularly?'

lop off   cut off
His head was lopped off for treason/His father lopped £50 a year off Michael's allowance for misbehaving.

prune   cut out what isn't necessary in written work
Your essay needs pruning severely.

sap   drain/exhaust s'o's strength/vitality
The London winter sapped their energy.

(n.) fool; silly person

root   1. stand unable to move through fascination/fear
He was/stood rooted to the pavement, terrified.
Fear rooted him to the step.
2. root about among = search among
3. root out = search for to get rid of
I'm going to go through my stamps and root out all the faded ones.
4. root round = inquire/search here and there
I'm going to root round and see if I can find any early editions of Dickens in Scotland.

(adj.) 1. His dislike of Bertie is deeply rooted.

(adj.) 2. He has a rooted (deep) objection to meat.

(n.) 1. The root (cause) of the matter/problem/trouble is . . .
Have you got to the root of the problem yet?

(n.) 2. take root = become established/establish itself
The idea of a police force took root in the nineteenth century.

tree   tree an animal/a man = force up a tree
The dogs treed the bear/man.

see **wood** below

trunk-call   (n.) long-distance phone call

wood   (n.) 1. can't see the wood for the trees = too close to the details to see s't as a whole

31

Des has so many minor problems to attend to in his business he's lost sight of the main problem – why they're losing money. He can't see the wood for the trees.

(n.) 2. They're not out of the wood yet = Even though they've solved some of their problems they've still got others to solve.

(n.) 3. What are you doing in this neck of the woods? (meaning here in an area/district/place where we don't usually see you)

wooden   (adj.) in behaviour/movement as if made of wood, therefore awkward/stiff/without expression
He had a very wooden way of playing the piano.
His movements were very wooden.
Tell him to relax and stop being so wooden.
Don't bring that fellow here again. He's so wooden; more like a robot, in fact, than a human being.

(adv. of this) woodenly

wooden-headed (adj.) stupid

Exercises

A. Give the correct answer to each sentence.

1. She has a . . . to green cheese.
   A root dislike   B root disliking   C rooted disliking   D rooted dislike
2. Poor Roger is
   A treading in the daisies   B pushing over the daisies
   C pushing up the daisies   C throwing over the daisies
3. Why don't you . . . Michael's book?
   A pull a leaf from   B take a leaf out of   C put a leaf in
   D have a leaf from
4. Stop looking at life . . .
   A with rosy glasses   B with rose-coloured glasses
   C through rose-coloured spectacles   D in rosy spectacles
5. Mr Hilton . . . the students who were lazy.
   A faded out   B branched off   C weeded out   D rooted round
6. Your trouble is you can't see
   A a wood for its trees   B the woods for trees
   C woods for trees   D the wood for the trees

7. I'm afraid Tom's taken . . .
   A the way of primroses   B the primrose path
   C the path of primroses   D to primrose path
8. Walter was innocent. The forged money must have been . . . him.
   A weeded for   B sown on   C grafted on   D planted on
9. Bill's neighbours are . . .
   A a thorn inside   B thorns inside   C a thorn in his side
   D thorns in the side
10. Where to get the money is . . .
    A the hard nut for cracking   B cracking hard nuts
    C a nut that will crack hard   D a hard nut to crack

B. By matching each word in 1. with a word in 2. find the ten pairs of
   words that are used in ten different idioms. Then use each idiom in a
   sentence.

1. path, rose, seeds, crack, thorn, weeds, lily, idea, daisy, olive
2. livered, plant, primrose, chain, branch, thorn, sow, widow's, chestnuts,
   side

C. Complete the sentences and idioms suitably.

   1. If only you . . . go for a walk you . . . some . . . in your cheeks.
   2. They . . . got on better if Eric . . . shown such a . . . objection to
      Ben.
   3. I wouldn't . . . if Victor . . . see . . . for the trees but he . . . see the
      problem only too clearly.
   4. If he hadn't . . . a few wild . . . in his youth, he . . . be so
      understanding towards young people now.
   5. Unless you . . . hedging and give a direct answer I . . . the police.
   6. If Jane . . . lost all that money on the . . . at Epsom last year she . . .
      to Paris this summer.
   7. The dogs . . . tree the cat if they . . . the chance.
   8. If John . . . over a new . . ., the headmaster would . . . everything he
      . . . to help him.
   9. I wish Lionel . . . use all that . . . language. It's too ornamental.
   10. The job . . . his energy if he . . . taken it.

D. (a) Which one of the four items forms or helps to form an idiom
      with the word that follows?   (b) Give the idiom fully, and
      explain it.

   1. A lily   B rose   C wall   D white   /thorn
   2. A willow   B blossom   C nut   D bush   /out
   3. A lane   B bush   C chair   D bed   /roses
   4. A bud   B sap   C leaf   D lop   /through

5. A lily	B rose	C trunk	D root	/window
6. A root	B wood	C fade	D branch	/round
7. A weed	B sow	C bud	D plant	/seeds
8. A arm	B neck	C leg	D head	/woods
9. A root	B thorn	C wooden	D willow	/headed
10. A lily	B rose	C daisy	D violet	/chain

The Body

arm

(n.) 1. in plural, up in arms = protesting angrily/ strongly
The students are up in arms over the new timetable.

(n.) 2. welcome s'o with open arms = welcome warmly

(adj.) keep s'o at arm's length = not become too friendly with s'o
She kept his friends at arm's length.

back

(n.) 1. break the back of a job/problem = complete the hardest part of
It took a month to break the back of the decorating.

(n.) 2. put one's back into s't = work one's hardest
He put his back into studying for the exam.

(n.) 3. put/get s'o's back up = make s'o angry

belly

(n.) have a bellyful of s't = have too much of s't one dislikes
We've had a bellyful of these films about violence.

bone

(n.) 1. It's been a bone of contention (between them) for some time now = a cause of argument/quarrelling

(n.) 2. have a bone to pick with s'o = a complaint
'I've (got) a bone to pick with you. Why don't you keep your room tidy?'

(n.) 3. make no bones about s't/doing s't = say/do/ without hesitation
They made no bones about it. They told him to go.

(adj.) bone-dry = completely dry

brain

(n.) 1. He's got football/murder/etc./on the brain = He talks/thinks/about nothing else.

(n.) 2. pick s'o's brains = find out and use s'o's ideas
The designers only invited him round to pick his brains.

(v.) brain s'o = hit s'o on the head/knock s'o out in this way

(adj.) 1. brainy/brainless person = clever/stupid person

(adj.) 2. crack-brained idea = stupid idea

cheek

(n.) 1. have one's tongue in one's cheek = say one thing and mean another/speak insincerely
He had his tongue in his cheek when he congratulated them.

(n.) 2. impudence/rudeness/sauce
Just like his cheek to ask for another £50.

(v. of this) cheek s'o = be cheeky/impudent/rude/saucy, and to give (s'o) cheek

chest

(n.) get s't off one's chest = confess/discuss a worry
'Well, get it off your chest. What's worrying you?'

ear

(n.) 1. be all ears = be very attentive/listen eagerly
They were all ears when he spoke of his detective work.

(n.) 2. up to one's ears (in work) = very busy

(n.) 3. have a good ear = have an accurate ear musically

(n.) 4. play by ear = play an instrument without using printed music

earmark

(v.) reserve s't (for oneself)
The librarian earmarked the most interesting novels for herself.

elbow

(n.) lift the elbow = drink too much

(adj.) 1. within elbow reach = nearby; within reach

(adj.) 2. elbow grease = hard work, mental or physical
Your homework is bad. You must use a little more elbow grease.

(adj.) 3. elbow room = room/space to move in

	(v.) elbow one's way/s'o aside = force/push one's way/s'o aside
eye	(n.) 1. give s'o the eye = wink at or indicate an interest in a member of the opposite sex
	(n.) 2. make eyes at = look lovingly at
	(n.) 3. (not) see eye to eye = (not) agree with completely
	(n.) 4. That's all my eye = That's all nonsense.
	(n.) 5. with an eye to = with the intention of/hoping for
	(v.) eye s'o/s't = look at/observe/watch/s'o/s't
eyebrows	(n.) That raised their eyebrows = That shocked/ surprised them.

Short questions

1. He got it off his chest means
   A He coughed   B He worried   C He talked   D He had an operation
2. A bone of contention is something
   A pleasant   B unpleasant   C friendly   D tasty
3. We see eye to eye = A We see well   B We speak frankly
   C We agree   D We look sideways
4. Crack-brained is   A stupid   B clever   C very clever   D tired
5. Explain 'He was all ears'.
6. Use 'cheek' in an idiom.

---

face	(n.) 1. lose face = be discredited/humiliated/made to look foolish Williams lost face at the office when he broke his promise to the staff.
	(n.) 2. tell s'o s't to his face = to a person directly (not behind s'o's back, q.v.), often s't unpleasant I told him to his face I didn't believe him.
	(n.) 3. keep a straight face = not to laugh although one wants to

He kept a straight face although he was laughing inwardly.

facer (n.) sudden (unexpected) difficulty/problem/question

finger (n.) 1. She could twist him round her little finger = She knew how to persuade him

(n.) 2. put one's finger on s't = find the/right word(s)/reason for s't
'Ah, you've put your finger on it. That's exactly what I/was trying to say/meant.'

(v.) examine with the fingers. He fingered the coin.

See **pie,** Food, p. 69

fist (n.) make a good fist of s't = do a difficult job well
He's made a very good fist of running that shop.

(adj.) tight-fisted = mean/miserly

foot/feet (n.) 1. put one's foot down = insist firmly/object/protest
He put his foot down when they tried to stay.

(n.) 2. put one's foot in it = make a mistake

(n.) 3. He had one foot in the grave = He was dying from old age (or illness).

(n.) 4. He fell on his feet = He had good luck at a time when he needed it.

(n.) 5. He learned to stand on his own two feet = He became confident/independent.

hair (n.) 1. Keep your hair on! = Keep calm/cool!

(n.) 2. He didn't turn a hair = He showed no signs of embarrassment/fear/surprise (when s't surprising happened).

(n.) 3. to split hairs = to argue over unimportant details/matters

hand at hand = near(by)/handy
The shops are quite handy.
in hand = 1. in reserve   2. under control   3. being attended to

1. I have £20 in hand.   2. He has things well in hand.   3. Your order is in hand and will be sent soon.
on hand = ready for sale/use
out of hand = out of control

(n.) 1. have a hand in = help to organize/plan
James had a hand in the/plot/scheme/new building.

(n.) 2. hand in glove with = in close relationship with
The lawyers and the police are/work hand in glove.

(n.) 3. live from hand to mouth = live from day to day
They've hardly any money. They live from hand to mouth.

head

(n.) 1. lose one's head = to panic/lose control of oneself (opposite = keep one's head)

(n.) 2. I can't make head or tail of it = I can't understand it at all.

(n.) 3. She has a good head for figures/languages, etc. = She has a natural ability for figures/languages, etc. (figures here = counting/mathematics/numbers)

heart

(n.) 1. have one's heart in the right place = be a kind person although it might not seem so
She sounds unkind but her heart's in the right place.

(n.) 2. set one's heart on doing/having s't = desire strongly
'She's set her heart on going to Paris.'

(n.) 3. Have a heart! = Be tolerant./Don't be hard-hearted (intolerant/unkind).

(n.) 4. lose heart = lose hope/become discouraged

see **sleeve**, Clothes, p. 51

heel

(n.) 1. take to one's heels/show a clean pair of heels = run away

(n.) 2. head over heels in love = completely in love

see **cool**, Weather, p. 85

knee   (n.) bring s'o to his knees = force s'o to agree/submit
                        They finally brought him to his knees, and he
                        resigned.

                        (adj.) weak-kneed = weak in character/not determined

---

Short questions

1. A facer is a   A person   B problem   C mirror   D mask
2. A mathematician has a good . . . for figures.
     A foot   B back   C head   D ear
3. She'd set her . . . on buying a house.
      A eye   B face   C heel   D heart
4. 'To take part in' uses an idiom of
     A hand   B foot   C arm   D fist
5. He was dying. Where was one foot?
6. Complete and explain the idiom with 'twist'.

---

knuckle   (n.) near the knuckle = almost/against morals/
                        indecent
                        That joke was a bit near the knuckle.

                        (v.) 1. knuckle down = settle down
                        You'd better knuckle down and do some work.

                        (v.) 2. knuckle under = do as one is told
                        They'd better knuckle under and keep quiet.

leg   (v.) 1. give s'o a leg up = help s'o

                        (v.) 2. not have a leg to stand on = not have anything
                        /in support of/to justify/an action/argument/attitude/
                        opinion
                        You haven't a leg to stand on. You had no cause to
                        be rude.

                        (v.) 3. leg it = run away
                        They legged it when they saw the police.

lips   (n.) 1. lick one's lips = show/the thought of/enjoyment
                        He licked his lips at the thought of having £2,000.

                        (n.) 2. I heard it from his own lips = He told me
                        himself

(n.) 3. (pay) lip-service = insincere agreement/
promise/respect
They praised the judge, but it was all lip-service.

mouth (n.) 1. down in the mouth = depressed/unhappy/
dejected

(n.) 2. put words in(to) s'o's mouth = make s'o
appear to have said s't they haven't said
'Stop putting words into my mouth. I never said
Patrick was a thief.'

(adj.) foul-mouthed = using dirty/foul language

neck (n.) 1. He got it in the neck = He/got into/had trouble.

(n.) 2. He stuck his neck out = He did/said s't that
made trouble.

(n.) 3. neck and neck = in close competition
Those two students are (going) neck and neck for
first place.

(n.) 4. He's/He gives me/a pain in the neck = He's
an irritating/a tiresome person.

(n.) 5. She had the neck/cheek/impudence to tell me
to shut up.

(v.) kiss (in the amatory sense)
They were necking in the cinema.

nose (n.) 1. pay through the nose = pay far more than the
value
He paid through the nose for those antique chairs.

(n.) 2. (right) under one's nose = in/front of/defiance
of/one
She winked at him right under my nose.

(v.) be inquisitive (adj.) nosey
Stop nosing (about) in my desk/being so nosey!

shin (v.) He shinned (climbed) up the drainpipe/tree.

shoulder (n.) have broad shoulders = able to stand/take a lot
of responsibility
Bill's got fairly broad shoulders. Running the family
business doesn't worry him.

(v. of this) 1. = to take (on) responsibility
Bill shouldered the responsibility when his father died.

(v.) 2. give s'o the cold shoulder = ignore/shun/snub s'o

(v.) 3. rub shoulders with = mix with people
In a university you rub shoulders with all kinds of people.

(v.) 4. shoulder s'o aside (*see* **elbow,** p. 36)

skeleton (n.) skeleton in the cupboard/the family skeleton = shameful secret in one's (family's) life
They say every family has a skeleton in the cupboard.

(adj.) skeleton key/staff = master key/minimum staff

skin (n.) 1. by the skin of one's teeth = only just manage
They/caught the bus/escaped/by the skin of their teeth.

(n.) 2. I nearly jumped out of my skin (with fright).

(adj.) 1. Keep your eyes skinned = Keep a sharp look-out.

(adj.) 2. His feelings are only skin-deep = not very deep

(adj.) 3. skinny = too thin in body

spine (adj.) spineless = very weak in character

Short questions

1. An inquisitive person is A lippy B throaty C nosey D skinny
2. Where has the family got a skeleton? In the
   A house B garden C kitchen D cupboard
3. Lip-service is something A insincere B sincere C to do with telephones D to do with lipstick
4. Which word makes an idiom with shoulder? A soft B cold C wet D dry
5. By giving him a . . . they helped him.
6. He got it in the . . . for being rude.

---

stomach

(n.) 1. have a strong/weak stomach = be a hardened/ an over-sensitive person
He has a weak stomach when it comes to murder films.

(n.) 2. have no stomach (enthusiasm) for s't
I've no stomach for politics these days.

(v.) How do you stomach/put up with/his rudeness?

throat

(n.) 1. cut one's own throat = do s't that will make a lot of trouble for oneself
If he marries Jane he'll be cutting his own throat.

(n.) 2. Don't jump down my throat every time I speak to you = Don't start an argument/a quarrel/ every time we talk.

(n.) 3. Don't keep forcing/shoving your ideas/opinions down other people's throats = Stop trying to make others agree with your ideas/opinions.

thumb

(n.) 1. under s'o's thumb = under s'o's authority/ influence
The son is completely under the mother's thumb.

(n.) 2. rule of thumb = method based on experience
He worked out how much wood he'd need by rule of thumb.

(n.) 3. He's all thumbs = He's very awkward.

(v.) He was thumbing (looking) through the directory.

(adj. of this) a well-thumbed book = much used

toe

(n.) 1. You have to be on your toes in that job = You have to be alert/wide awake.

(n.) 2. tread on s'o's toes = upset s'o by criticizing/ questioning his beliefs/ideas/opinions
I wish he'd stop treading on his uncle's toes. He knows the old man doesn't see eye to eye (*q.v.*) with him.

(v.) toe the line = do as one is told
In the army you have to toe the line.

tooth

(n.) 1. He's a bit long in the tooth = old

(n.) 2. She/has a sweet tooth/likes sweet things.

(n.) 3. in the teeth of = in spite of (opposition)
She married him in the teeth of disapproval.

(n.) 4. show one's teeth = show hostility
The moment they insulted him he showed his teeth.

tongue

(n.) 1. Hold your tongue! = Keep quiet!

(n.) 2. It was a slip of the tongue. I meant two not
three = a mistake in speaking/writing

(adj.) tongue-tied = too nervous/shy to speak

feeling/mind/sense/soul/spirit

(n.) 1. He hasn't much feeling (sympathy/
understanding).

(n.) 2. No hard feelings, I hope = I hope you're not
angry with me for what's happened.

(n.) She spoke her mind = She spoke frankly.

(n.) He's taken leave of his senses = He's gone mad.

(v.) He sensed (realized) that s't was wrong.

(n.) 1. She has no soul = no artistic/emotional
feeling.

(n.) 2. There wasn't a soul (person) to be seen.

(n.) 3. You can't call your soul your own in their
house =You have to do what they want, not what
you want.

(n.) 'What spirit (mood) was it said in?' 'Oh, in the
right (a friendly/helpful) spirit, I think.' 'Well, it was
taken in the wrong spirit here. He should be more
careful with his remarks.'

Exercises

A. Which part of the body is used in an idiom meaning the following?

1. to show enjoyment
2. doing as one is told
3. finishing the hardest part of a job
4. reserving something
5. being old

6. being under someone's control
7. being wide-awake
8. to keep quiet
9. to have no enthusiasm for
10. to pay an excessive price

B. Which of these parts of the body are used in an idiom meaning the following?

1. to have too much of something
   A bone   B belly   C brain   D back
2. to talk about only one subject
   A arm   B brain   C cheek   D chest
3. to lose someone's good opinion
   A face   B heart   C leg   D mouth
4. to try to make someone agree with your ideas
   A throat   B nose   C knuckle   D tongue
5. to do something against opposition
   A heart   B heel   C teeth   D tongue

C. Complete the idioms correctly.

1. She's very unsympathetic. She hasn't much . . .
   A knowing   B calling   C feeling   D mind
2. What . . . did he make the remark in?
   A form   B soul   C spirit   D mind
3. He put his . . . into passing the exam.
   A hand   B foot   C head   D back
4. She put her . . . on it when she described John as weak-kneed.
   A hand   B finger   C arm   D eye
5. He was looking very . . . in the mouth when I saw him.
   A sad   B low   C down   D sour
6. Such an awkward boy! He's all . . .
   A hands   B feet   C arms   D thumbs
7. Don't . . . down my throat because I've told you the truth.
   A rush   B jump   C leap   D go
8. You can't . . . your soul your own in this office.
   A name   B have   C own   D call
9. They'll have to . . . the line here!
   A foot   B leg   C heel   D toe
10. Don't believe him. He usually has his tongue in his . . .
    A mouth   B cheek   C teeth   D throat

D. Complete as sentences by including the words in brackets.

1. The audience their rushed for the exits. (heads, and, lost)

2. He soon his they disagreed with him. (when, showed, teeth)
3. She hasn't a leg on. (got, stand, to)
4. His intonation is excellent. He a good. (ear, has, very)
5. Mary keeps arm's (at, length, everyone)
6. If Jim doesn't soon fail his exam. (he'll, down, knuckle)
7. Margaret no telling him to go. (about, made, bones)
8. They the plane by the of teeth. (caught, their, skin)
9. He doesn't make a the tongue. (of, slip, often)
10. I've seen him up a tree in half. (minute, shin, a)

E. Complete with suitable prepositions or adverbs.

1. She flirted with him . . . my very nose.
2. His remarks usually get their backs . . .
3. She eventually brought James . . . his knees.
4. We've got a bone to pick . . . your brother.
5. Our carpenter usually goes . . . rule . . . thumb.
6. Stop putting words . . . my mouth!
7. The drivers are . . . in arms over the company's offer.
8. It's good to rub shoulders . . . various people.
9. The reference books are . . . elbow reach.
10. I warned you not to stick your neck . . .

Clothes

apron   (adj.) He's tied to his mother's apron strings = He's too dependent on her (either as a youth or adult). Also to his 'wife's apron strings'.

boot   (n.) 1. get/give s'o/the boot = dismiss/be dismissed from (kicked out of) a job

(n.) 2. give s'o a good boot = kick s'o hard
Jimmy needs a good boot. He's bone lazy.

(n.) 3. The boot's on the other foot (now) = The situation is reversed.
When Frank was the boss he made life very unpleasant for George but now the boot's on the other foot. George is the boss and Frank has to look out.

(n.) 4. luggage compartment in a car

(v.) boot out = dismiss from (kick out of) a job/place
He booted his son out of the home.

cap   (n.) 1. She set her cap at him = She determined to marry him.

(n.) 2. He went to the boss cap in hand = He went to the boss humbly.

(n.) 3. Where/If the cap fits (then wear it); used without the ending = If a remark is true, then it applies.
'She said Jack was very foxy.' 'Well, if the cap fits.'

(v.) cap a joke/remark/story = make/tell a better one
Roy told a very funny story about an Irishman, but Geoff capped it with one about a Welshman.

cloth   *see* **coat**, p. 48

clothes	(adj.) clothes-horse = frame for airing/drying clothes on
coat	(n.) 1. cut one's coat according to one's cloth = live within one's income Eve can't afford to go on world cruises. She has to cut her coat according to her cloth so she goes to Europe instead. (n.) 2. coat (layer) of paint. But a coating (very thin layer) of dust (n.) 3. turncoat = s'o who changes sides to his own advantage Smithson's a turncoat. He left his own political party and went over to the opposition. Apparently they offered to make him a minister if they win the next election.
glove	see **hand**, The Body, p. 38
hat	(n.) 1. Keep it under your hat = Keep it secret. (n.) 2. I take my hat off to James = I admire/respect James for his actions/attitude. (n.) 3. talk through one's hat = talk nonsense Don't listen to Ray. He doesn't know anything about chemistry. He's talking through his hat. (adj.) old hat = old-fashioned/out of fashion Films with happy endings are old hat today.
jacket	(n.) 1. dust jacket = loose paper cover that protects a book (n.) 2. potatoes in their jackets = potatoes baked in their skins
shirt	(n.) 1. bet/put one's shirt on s't = be quite sure about a project/scheme (The idiom comes from betting all one's money on a horse; also 'to lose one's shirt'.) 'They'll use your plan, Mike. You can put your shirt on it.' Jack put his shirt on 'Whistling Willie' in the 4 o'clock race. It lost, of course, and Jack lost his shirt.

(n.) 2. He hasn't a shirt to his back = He hasn't any money/He's very poor.

(n.) 3. Keep your shirt on! = Keep your hair on! (*see* **hair**, The Body, p. 38)

(n.) 4. He'd give you the shirt off his back = He's very generous.

(adj.) shirty = bad-tempered/irritable

shoe

(n.) 1. I wouldn't (want to) be in his/her shoes = I wouldn't want his/her difficulties/problems.

(n.) 2. shoestring = a very small budget
They made the film on a shoestring.

skirt

(n.) 1. a bit of skirt (vulgar usage) = a girl/woman

(n.) 2. the outskirts of a town = the beginnings or outer edges

(v.) to skirt the edge of s't = be on or go/move along its edge
The police skirted the field to reach the river quickly.

sock

(n.) 1. Pull your socks up! = Behave better/Show an improvement.

(n.) 2. Put a sock in it! = Shut up (it = your mouth)

(n.) 3. a sock (blow) in the face/on the jaw, etc.

(v. of this) hit s'o
He socked Bill on the jaw, so Bill socked him back.

tie

(n.) 1. black tie/white tie = dinner jacket/tails (*see* **Animals,** Domestic, p. 10)
'What are we supposed to wear tonight, black tie or white tie?'

(n.) 2. wear an/the old school tie = be a former pupil of a public or grammar school

trousers

(n.) wear the trousers = be the dominant person in a family/marriage
'Who wears the trousers in that family?' 'The wife does I'm afraid, though sometimes I think it's the mother-in-law.'

Short questions

1. You have to cut your coat according to your
   A taste B size C cloth D tailor
2. Give someone a good boot and he is
   A pleased B tired C ungrateful D hurt
3. Billy, shut up! Put a . . . in it!
   A glove B sock C hand D sack
4. I prefer potatoes in their
   A hats B coats C jackets D vests
5. Use 'shoes' in an idiom.
6. What do you talk through if you're talking nonsense?

Details

belt

(n.) 1. hit (s'o) below the belt = behave/fight unfairly
Even though George doesn't like Peter, it was (hitting) below the belt to tell the manager that Peter always comes late.

(n.) 2. give s'o a (good) belt = hit s'o
(v. of this) 1. = belt s'o

(n.) 3. tighten one's belt = economize, or go without food
'We'll have to tighten our belts, gentlemen. The firm's lost a lot of money this year.'

(v.) 2. Belt up! = Shut up!

button

(adj.) buttoned up = arranged/fixed/settled (*see* **sew,** p. 52)
Jackson Motors are going in with Smith Brothers. The directors have got it all buttoned up.

buttonhole

(n.) flower worn in the buttonhole
'That's a nice buttonhole you've got there, Jimmy.'

(v.) wait to stop s'o in order to talk to him
'It was twenty minutes before he managed to buttonhole the headmaster in the corridor.

collar

(n.) 1. get hot under the collar = get angry/upset
'It's no good getting hot under the collar over what the critics say about your play.'

50

(n.) 2. grab s'o by the collar = seize s'o roughly
They grabbed the thief by the collar and took him to
the police station.
(v. of this) collar. They collared him and took him
away.

pocket   (n.) 1. be in/out of/pocket = have made/lost money
on/over s't
He was £5 in/out of/pocket over the sale of his car.

(n.) 2. put one's pride in one's pocket = swallow
one's pride = not be too proud to do s't one doesn't
like doing
'Put your pride in your pocket and work as a waiter
during the holiday. It won't hurt you.'

(n.) 3. Frank's always ready to put his hand in his
pocket = Frank's always ready to give/spend money.

(n.) 4. pick s'o's pocket/have one's pocket picked =
steal s't from s'o's/have s't stolen from one's/pocket
(n. of this) 5. a pickpocket

(v.) 1. pocket one's pride (as above)

(v.) 2. take s't for oneself (often dishonestly)
The manager pocketed the bonus that should have
been shared out among the staff.

sleeve   (n.) 1. have s't up one's sleeve = have a secret idea/
plan ready for use
'What's Baker going to do with all that land he owns?'
'I don't know but I'm sure he's got s't up his sleeve.'

(n.) 2. Philip's laughing up his sleeve = He's secretly
amused.
But, laughing up one's sleeve at s'o = secretly scorning

(n.) 3. roll one's sleeves up = work hard
'Jack's not afraid to roll his sleeves up.'

(n.) 4. wear one's heart on one's sleeve = show one's
emotions openly (often used negatively)
Margaret doesn't wear her heart on her sleeve, so
Roy doesn't know she's in love with him.

zip   (n.) a zip-up = s't that enlivens a person
'Have a glass of sherry. That'll give you a zip-up.'

(v. of this) to zip s'o up

Verbs and Other Forms

cut
1. *see* **coat** 1., p. 48

2. cut it fine = leave oneself very little of s't (material, money, time, etc.); often used with pretty/rather/very
You've cut it pretty fine. There's only one tin of paint left to do the kitchen with.

3. cut out for/to be = have the qualities for a certain career
Elizabeth's cut out to be a doctor/nurse/teacher.

4. cut s't short = end s't by shortening it
They cut the ceremony short so the guests could catch their plane.

hem in
enclose/surround; often used in the passive.
The two men were hemmed in by the police.

iron out
solve (smooth out) difficulties/problems

seamy
the seamy side of life = the unpleasant side of life (crime/poverty/vice, etc.)

sew
sewn up = buttoned up (q.v.)

stitch
(n.) 1. not have a stitch on = be naked

(n.) 2. A stitch in time (saves nine). A proverb = A little work now may save a lot of work later on.
'I'll fill that crack in the wall now before the whole wall splits. A stitch in time.'

strait-laced
(adj.) puritanical/very strict moral attitude

Exercises

A. Rewrite with the idioms corrected.

1. He hit Jack on the belt.
2. Bill went to the manager cap in the hand.
3. The lawyers have got everything buttoned on.

4. I was £10 out from my pocket over that sale.
5. That drive in the country zipped my aunt off.
6. Peter was shoed out of his job yesterday.
7. Mary helped us to iron down our problems.
8. John's still tired of his wife's apron strings.
9. You've cut very fine. We've only five minutes to get there.
10. Jim's always willing to hand over his pocket if it'll help.

B. Give the idiom which correctly completes these sentences.

1. There's a very fine . . . of dust over all the furniture.
2. You can put . . . I'm certain you'll get the job.
3. They say a stitch . . .
4. Betty doesn't wear . . . She's emotional, nonetheless.
5. The thieves were in the wood. The police had got them . . .
6. Her moral attitude is very severe, isn't it? I find her extremely . . .
7. Michael's story was clever but Frank was able to . . . with a cleverer one.
8. I could see the linen drying on a . . .
9. The father's the boss in that home. The wife certainly doesn't . . .
10. I'm tired of your laziness. You'll have to . . .

C. Complete the sentences, including an idiom for the word(s) in brackets.

1. I wouldn't care . . . his . . . (problems)
2. She refused . . . and work as a maid. (humble herself)
3. They weren't looking forward . . . (economizing)
4. He threatened . . . Alan . . . (kick hard)
5. It's no good . . . the thieves in the day time. (seize roughly)
6. Alice warned Jane not . . . at George. (aim at, marriage)
7. There's no point in . . . the boss if he's already refused to talk to you. (wait to talk to)
8. The firm is believed . . . (a secret plan)
9. Without . . . you won't achieve very much. (work hard)
10. You'll have to stop . . . when we're going by train.
    It's too much of a rush to the station. (leave very little time)

D. Write ten sentences using each word or word group once only in, or as, an idiom. Do not change the form of the word(s).

1. cap 2. to hem 3. sleeve 4. cut out 5. stitch on 6. cut it
7. boot's on 8. cap fits 9. buttonhole 10. shirt off

Colours

All the words of colour in this section are used as adjectives unless marked otherwise.

ashen   *see* **grey,** p. 56

black   1. give s'o a black look = look angrily at s'o

2. be black and blue = be badly bruised/have many bruises

3. I'd like it in black and white = I'd like it in writing (not just a spoken form; usually an agreement, a contract, statement, or other printed form of s't).

4. black eye = bruise round eye from a blow

5. *see* **sheep,** Animals (Domestic), p. 6

(n.) 1. blackleg = s'o who agrees to work when union members are on strike

(n.) 2. blacklist = (a) State list of dangerous political enemies (b) list kept by businesses/organizations of unreliable firms, customers or others (often used in an imaginary sense).
Jack won't get an overdraft. He's on the bank's black-list.

(v. of this) 1. blacklist s'o

(v.) 2. blackball s'o = vote against s'o joining a club/group/society

(v.) 3. black out = (a) cut off electrical power in a district/town
A strike by power men blacked out London for two hours last night.
(b) lose consciousness/one's memory/for a period

(n.) 3. black-out = power/mental failure or fainting

Brian's had another black-out. He can't remember a thing.
Nancy had a black-out. She was unconscious for two hours.

(v.) 4. to black goods = refusal by dockers, railmen, etc., to load/unload goods from a firm where there is a strike.

blackmail

(v.) threaten to reveal s'o's shameful secret unless he pays money

(n.) of person who does this = blackmailer

blue

1. blue cinema/films/jokes = obscene c/f/j

2. once in a blue moon = once in a lifetime/very rarely
'How often am I likely to win on the football pools?'
'Once in a blue moon, I should think.'

3. in a blue funk = very frightened
Don was in a blue funk before he met Jennie's father.

4. feel/look blue = feel/look depressed (*see* 'down in the mouth', **The Body**, p. 41, and 'fit of the blues' below)

5. blue with (the) cold = either really or figuratively blue with cold

6. out of the blue = suddenly/unexpectedly
Mary inherited the money out of the blue.
Tom turned up out of the blue after five years.

(n.) 1. He's true blue = He's a loyal friend/member of a group/political party.

(n.) 2. He's a true blue = loyal (Conservative) Party member

(n.) 3. He's got a fit of the blues = He's depressed.

(v.) blue = spend money extravagantly/foolishly (squander it)
Leslie's aunt gave him £300 and he blued the lot in a week.

brown

1. browned off = fed up (also cheesed off, *see* **Food**, p. 65)
There was nothing to do, and Harry was feeling browned off.

2. as brown as a berry = very sun-tanned

green

1. be green = be inexperienced/untrained/easily deceived
He's still green. He only got the job last week.
She was so green she lent him £500.

(n. of this) a greenhorn

2. feel/look green = feel/look ill
'You're looking very green, Des.' 'The way this ship is rolling, I feel green.'

3. turn green, also = look ill
'You've turned green.'

4. get/give s'o/the green light = get/give s'o/ permission to go ahead with a plan/project
'We've got the green light. The Council have told us to start building the new hospital.'

5. green-eyed = jealous
She looked at Vera in a very green-eyed way.

6. green with envy
She was green with envy when her sister got a new dress.

7. green fingers = skill as a gardener
She's got green fingers. She can make anything grow.

8. green stuff = green vegetables or vegetation

9. the green/Emerald Isle = Ireland

(n.) greens = (a) green vegetables (b) grassy spaces = village greens/bowling greens/putting greens (for golf)

grey

1. go/turn grey = become grey-haired

(v. of this) = grey; usually in continuous
He's greying slowly.

2. grey matter = intelligence (*see* **brainy**, The Body, p. 36)
'Lionel hasn't much grey matter, unlike Bernard – plenty of grey matter there.'

3. go/look/turn grey (or ashen) with illness/worry

(n.) grey beard = old man
Victor's a grey beard (these days).

Short questions

1. Browned off = A fed up   B sunburnt   C thoughtful   D tired
2. The disreputable member of the family is the
   A brown goat   B blue snake   C black sheep   D green finger
3. The Emerald Isle is   A off South America   B imaginary
   C where emeralds are mined   D near Britain
4. Intelligence uses the idiom of colour
   A green   B grey   C blue   D brown
   What is the idiom?
5. What is a grey beard?
6. Use 'black-out' in an idiom.

---

pink

1. in the pink = very well/very healthy

2. be (a little/slightly) pink = (slightly) left wing
politically

3. go/turn pink (with embarrassment/shame); often
used instead of go/turn red/scarlet (*see* **red, scarlet,**
below)
She turned/went pink (with shame) when they caught
her looking through the keyhole.

4. to see pink elephants = to have too much to drink
'I think Basil saw a few pink elephants last night.'

(n.) pinks = pink and other coloured flowers from
type of garden plant
He bought her a bunch of pinks.

(v.) knocking sound in car engine; due to a fault
'It was pinking like mad this morning.' 'It's probably
that cheap petrol you buy.'

purple

1. He became/went purple (with rage).

2. purple patch(es) = in a prose passage or poem the
parts very rich (even over-rich) in style
Terence knows most of the purple patches in
Shakespeare by heart.

red

1. be red with anger/embarrassment/shame

2. go/turn red (with a/e/s). The words in brackets
are optional when the reason is clear from the context.

57

3. be a/go/turn/Red = be a/go/turn Communist

4. be in/get/go into the red = be in/get/go into debt
also get out of the red
He's/The firm's/They're heavily in the red.

5. to see red = to become/get angry
Arthur saw red when the shop overcharged him.

6. put down/put/roll/run out the red carpet (for s'o) =
give s'o an official or very warm (enthusiastic) welcome
They put out the red carpet for the British trade
delegation in Chile.

7. catch s'o/be caught red-handed = in the act
The headmaster caught Joyce red-handed in his
study. She was looking at the exam papers.

8. see the red light = see danger in time
Jack saw the red light and gave up smoking before it
was too late.

9. paint the town red = celebrate noisily/wildly
They painted the town red the night they passed the
exam.

10. a red herring = an attempt to draw attention
away from the main facts with an unimportant/
unrelated/detail
The Prime Minister's reference to unemployment was
a red herring. He wanted to get away from the trade
figures.

11. (like) a red rag (to a bull) = a cause of anger
'Don't talk to Hugh about rising prices. It's like a
red rag.'

12. a red-letter day = a very important day in s'o's
life
Saturday's a red-letter day for Frank. He's getting
engaged.

13. red tape = too many formalities/rules and
regulations
'There's too much red tape when you deal with some
of these government departments. How many this,
how many that? Fill in form A in triplicate. Write in
block capitals only. You know the sort of thing.'
'Only too well. I happen to be a civil servant.'

(v.) redden = blush

scarlet   go/turn scarlet = go/turn bright/very red with embarrassment/shame

white

1. Her face/She turned/went white = Her face/She turned/went pale with fear/shock/at the news.
also: She turned/went as white as a sheet = Her face/She 'changed colour (*see* **colour,** p. 60).

2. bleed white = cause to lose strength/wealth
Some people say we're bled white by taxes.

3. white elephant *see* **elephant**, Animals (Wild), p. 15

4. fly/show/wave the white flag = give in/surrender
Joe's been waving the white flag. He's ready to apologize to Audrey.

5. a white lie = a lie told to avoid hurting s'o's feelings; or a polite or comforting lie
Brian told Phyllis a white lie. He said he hadn't called because he'd been too busy. Actually he'd forgotten.

6. white paper = British Government report issued publicly

(v.) whitewash = attempt to cover up s'o's mistakes (a business/country/group/person)
The directors tried to whitewash the situation but the manager had obviously told the Press that the firm was in the red.

(n.) white of egg; the white of an/one egg; the whites of two (etc.) eggs (for cooking)
She used white of egg/the whites of three eggs.

Short questions

1. A red rag causes
   A anger   B pleasure   C doubt   D fear
2. A white paper is a
   A newspaper   B handkerchief   C published report   D blank page
3. They were angry = They went
   A blue   B green   C grey   D purple
4. 'Very well' = A pink   B looking pink
   C in the pink   D pinking

5. Explain 'They put out the red carpet'.

6. Use 'white' in an idiom, and explain the idiom.

---

yellow

1. He's yellow = He's cowardly/a coward.

2. also: He has a yellow streak.

3. the Yellow Book/Pages = in British towns a 'phone book of trades and occupations. It is printed on yellow paper.

4. the yellow Press = papers which try to give news in a way that will arouse feelings (their favourite words include 'shock, surprise, sensation, drama').

(v.) The leaves are/were yellowing (=turning yellow or brown)

Verbs and Other Forms

colour

1. exaggerate/misrepresent
The newspapers (greatly) coloured the story.

(adj. of this) It was a highly coloured story.

2. blush
She coloured when he caught her at the keyhole.

(n.) 1. change colour (*see* **white,** p. 59 no. 1.)

(n.) 2. give/lend colour to = help/seem to prove
Her empty purse gave/lent colour to her story of having no money.

(n.) 3. have a high colour = have a red complexion

(adj.) 1. colour-blind = unable to tell the difference between certain colours

(adj.) 2. He's off colour today = He's depressed/unwell.

(n.) 4. He's/She's sailing under false colours = He's/She's pretending to be what he/she isn't.

(n.) 5. see s'o/s't in his/its true colours = see s'o/s't as he/it really is (n.) 6. show one's/oneself in one's/true colours = show one's real self

(n.) 7. pass an exam with flying colours = pass it very successfully

(n.) 8. colours = flag of a regiment/ship

colourful   (adj.) bright/exciting/gay/lively/vivid
a colourful idea/life/person/piece of music/scene/story/style, etc.

colourless   (adj.) opposite of above

shade   (n.) 1. 'What is the exact shade (variety) of meaning of that verb?' 'It's not easy to say. It has so many shades of meaning.'

(n.) 2. be/leave/put in the shade = be/leave/put s'o/s't into a lesser/an unimportant/position (to eclipse)
The new jetliner has put all its rivals in the shade.

Exercises

A. Choose the correct answer to each sentence.

1. A business that is in debt is
   A on the red   B in the black   C in the red   D going red
2. A coward has a
   A blue streak   B green line   C grey line   D yellow streak
3. A person who is depressed is
   A off colour   B out of colour   C colourless   D in the shade
4. To lose your memory for a while is to
   A be browned off   B blue it   C black out   D turn pink
5. When someone gives you the O.K. you get the
   A green eye   B pink elephant   C red herring   D green light
6. Unreliable customers go on the
   A black list   B white paper   C yellow pages   D purple patch
7. A loyal friend is   A true green   B pure pink   C white of egg
   D true blue
8. People are listed by their occupations in the
   A green pages   B blue book   C white paper   D yellow book
9. The newspapers *exaggerated* the story.
   A reddened   B coloured   C shaded   D blacked

10. 'I was in a . . . funk.'
    A green   B brown   C blue   D red

B. What is the colour associated with an idiom for each of the following?
   Say or write out the idiom.
   1. Spending money extravagantly.
   2. Wanting a printed document.
   3. Getting old.
   4. Very seldom.
   5. Being ready to give in.
   6. An unexpected happening.
   7. Seeing a danger before it is too late.
   8. Draining someone of their wealth.
   9. A person with little experience.
   10. Found breaking the law.

C. Which item (A, B, C or D) correctly forms an idiom with each of the
   following?

   1. He's . . . under false colours.
      A riding   B walking   C sailing   D flying
   2. John tried to join the ABC club but he was . . .
      A blackballed   B blacklisted   C blacked   D blacked out
   3. Considerately he told Mary a . . . lie.
      A blue   B grey   C yellow   D white
   4. She passed her exam with . . . colours.
      A floating   B flapping   C running   D flying
   5. He looked . . . with cold
      A grey   B blue   C green   D pink
   6. They showed themselves in their . . . colours.
      A true   B first   C actual   D own
   7. That white paper was an attempt to . . . the Ministry's mistakes.
      A yellow paint   B green eye   C whitewash   D red tape
   8. 'Rough seas always make me feel . . .'
      A green   B red   C red   D purple
   9. The shock at seeing the accident made her turn quite . . .
      A blue   B white   C red   D black
   10. No wonder he saw . . . elephants after all that whisky.
      A blue   B red   C pink   D white

D. Complete each of the following with an idiom and any other words
   you think are necessary.

   1. 'You . . .' 'Yes, I feel thoroughly depressed.'
   2. 'She . . .' 'Yes, she's always been red-faced.'

3. It's an exciting story, full of . . . ideas.
4. During the strike the management got in some   ., who fought with the union members, and one union man gave one of the . . . a . . .
5. 'How would you explain that word? What is its exact . . . .?'
6. Jack's as . . . I've never seen anyone so sun-tanned.
7. Bill . . . for days now. He wants to stop the quarrel but Edith won't take any notice.
8. In about a week's time you . . . to go ahead. The firm intends to use your plan.
9. 'Is he Red?' 'Nothing as extreme as that . . ., that's all.'
10. His uncle, who died last year, . . . He could make anything grow.'

Food

apple

(n.) 1. the apple of s'o's eye = greatly loved
She was the apple of her father's eye.

(adj.) 1. in apple-pie order = in perfect order/very tidy

(adj.) 2. upset the apple cart = disorganize/spoil a plan/situation
When Ann suggested giving a party at home, it completely upset the apple cart. Her father got quite angry.

bacon

(n.) save one's bacon = escape s't (death/injury/ telling off)/manage to avoid failure
He saved his bacon by running across the rooftops.
The ladder saved his bacon during the fire.
His cheerful manner saved his bacon at the interview.

beans

(n.) 1. I haven't a bean = I've no money at all.

(n.) 2. full of beans = very energetic/lively
Harry's full of beans. One of the liveliest people I know.

beef

(n.) muscle/strength
Frank's pretty strong. Enough beef there. But Tim could do with more beef/a bit of beef.

(adj. of this) beefy

biscuit

(n.) take the biscuit. This is applied to behaviour or a remark/suggestion that is far-fetched/ridiculous.
Ada's begun pretending she's a millionairess. That really takes the biscuit.

bread

(n.) 1. take the bread out of s'o's mouth = take away s'o's job or chance of making a living

The men at the factory said the new automatic equipment could take the bread out of a good many mouths.

(n.) 2. Paul knows which side his bread is buttered = He knows where things are best/most advantageous/ for him.

(n.) 3. How does he earn his bread and butter? = What does he do for a living?
Designing furniture is his bread and butter.
see **loaf,** p. 71; **toast,** p. 69

broth	*see* **cook,** p. 70
butter	(n.) 1. He/She looks as if butter wouldn't melt in his/ her mouth = He/She looks innocent/mild. (n.) 2. 'You want butter on both sides, don't you?' (*see* **jam,** p. 67) (v.) butter s'o up = flatter s'o He buttered her up with various compliments.
butter-fingers	(n.) s'o who can't hold or catch things well with the hands. Said as 'Butter-fingers!' or 'He's/She's a butter-fingers.'
cake	(n.) 1. You can't have your cake and eat it = You can't enjoy/have two things that are a contradiction. You want to keep buying new clothes, and save your money, but you can't have your cake and eat it. (n.) 2. go/sell like hot cakes = sell very quickly Those half-price shirts are selling like hot cakes.
carrot	(n.) attraction/bait As manager you're working all the time. The carrot, of course, is £6,000 a year.
cauliflower	(adj.) a cauliflower ear = a damaged/mis-shapen ear; often seen on boxers.
cheese	(adj.) cheesed off = fed up (*see* **browned off,** Colours, p. 55)
corny	(adj.) inferior/old-fashioned/unoriginal (used critically) A corny film/joke/novel/play/person

He's very corny. Always says the same old things.

cucumber (n.) be as cool as a cucumber = behave calmly in a dangerous/difficult situation (*see also* **head,** The Body, p. 39)
A wheel came off his car but Peter was as cool as a cucumber.

gooseberry (n.) play gooseberry = be present when two people want to be alone (often used in the negative)
John made an excuse not to walk with Dan and Mary. He wasn't going to play gooseberry.

grapes (n.) Sour grapes/It's sour grapes. This is a comment s'o makes when s'o says s't is no good, or not to his liking, because presumably, he can't have it himself (from Aesop's fable of the fox, the crow and the grapes).
'I don't care if Margaret gets a fur coat. Anyway, I don't like fur.' 'Sour grapes!'

grapevine (n.) hear s't on/over/through the grapevine = hear s't from/through an unofficial source
'How do you know Jackson is leaving?' 'I heard it over the grapevine.'

Short questions

1. Her remark took the
   A carrot   B apple   C biscuit   D cucumber
2. Peter's full of
   A bacon   B broth   C cake   D beans
3. 'Sour grapes!' Mary said because Jane was
   A ill   B greedy   C pretending   D slow
4. Cauliflower is applied to
   A feet   B hands   C noses   D ears
5. What does 'corny' mean?
6. Use 'cheese' in an idiom. Explain the idiom.

---

ham (adj.) ham actor = one whose technique is weak or obvious; also used as a noun: He's an awful ham.

jam   (n.) to want jam on it = to want everything
'I want a house, a car, a yacht, and —'
'You want jam on it, don't you?' (= butter on both sides, q.v.)

mincemeat   (n.) 1. make mincemeat of an idea/a plan/a theory = show it to be useless/worthless
The science department made mincemeat of the new atomic theory.

(n.) 2. make mincemeat of a person (in a fight) = defeat completely

mushroom   (n.) made of wood to put in socks when darning.

(v.) mushroom (out/up) = expand/grow rapidly (e.g. shops/towns)
The town began mushrooming out in all directions.

peas   (n.) in the simile: as like as two peas, or, like two peas in a pod = exactly alike; identical

pepper   (v.) throw a quantity of things at; question thoroughly
They peppered the burglars with everything they could throw.
They peppered him with questions about South America.

pepper-and-salt   (n.) clothing material pattern of small checks, usually black, or brown, and white

peppery   (adj.) hot-tempered

plum   (n.) 1. the best of a collection of things
The paintings fetched £200,000. As usual the American buyers got the plums (of the collection).

(adj.) a plum job = a very good job
(the predicative adjective of this) plummy

raspberry   (n.) get (give s'o) a/the raspberry = gesture/noise/ statement of contempt/disapproval/dislike/refusal
I tried to sell my old car to a dealer but he gave me a raspberry. He said it wasn't even fit for scrap metal.

salt	(v.) salt away = save money Tom salts away a few pounds every month. (n.) take s't s'o says with a grain/pinch of salt = consider it exaggerated 'Bob says he once shot twelve lions.' 'I know. We've always taken that with a grain of salt.'
soup	(n.) be in the soup = be in trouble
spice	(v.) flavour a story with adventure/excitement/humour, etc. I like the way he spices his stories with amusing remarks.
sugar	(v.) sugar the pill = use pleasant encouragement to get s'o to accept/do s't unpleasant (e.g. job/news) The college doubled the amount of homework but they sugared the pill with an extra half-holiday a week.
sugary	(adj.) music/play/story that is too sweet (sentimental).
tripe	(n.) idea/music/play/story/talk that is nonsense/worthless (often with 'a load/lot of' and 'utter', i.e. absolute) That film was just a load of tripe. I wish he'd stop talking tripe. 'What did you think of that novel?' 'Tripe, utter tripe!'

Details

core	(n.) 1. (get to) the core of the matter = (get to) the centre/heart/root of an argument/a discussion/subject, etc. (n.) 2. rotten to the core = thoroughly rotten (s'o/s't)
fat	(n.) The fat's in the fire now = The fact/news of s't is now known, and is going to cause anger/trouble.
fruit	(n.) product/result Her book was the fruit of several years' work.

	(adj.) fruitful = profitable/having good results
meal	(n.) make a meal out of s't = treat s't trivial/as very important/at great length When George explained how a tap worked he really made a meal out of it.
meat	(n.) 1. One man's meat is another man's poison = What suits one man, doesn't suit another. (n.) 2. Cowboy stories are meat and drink to Charles = s't he likes very much.
mustard	(n.) in the simile: as keen as mustard = very keen
oven	It's like an oven in here = It's too warm in here. *cf.* **toast,** below
pancake	(n.) in the simile: as flat as a pancake
pickle	(n.) be in (a bit of) a pickle = be in difficulty (-ties)/trouble (adj.) be pickled = be drunk/intoxicated
pie	(n.) 1. have a finger in the pie = have a hand in (*q.v.*) (n.) 2. as easy as pie = very easy
pip	(n.) give one the pip = annoy/depress/disturb one Roy gives me the pip. He always knows so much. (v.) pip s'o at the post = defeat at the last moment Humes, the building firm, thought they were getting the skyscraper contract, but they were pipped at the post by Clarkes.
toast	(n.) 'I'm/It's as warm as toast = pleasantly warm (usually in cold weather) *cf.* **oven,** above

---

Short questions

1. That actor is a complete
   A cheese B plum C ham D salt

2. The town mushroomed =
   A shrank B grew very quickly C got very dirty D became crowded
3. In the soup = In:
   A the money B the way C danger D trouble
4. As . . . as mustard
   A slow B thick D keen D fit
5. Explain: He gives me the pip.
6. Give a sentence using 'pie' as an idiom.

Verbs and Other Forms

bake

(v.) The pitch was baked = made hard by the sun's heat

(adj.) half-baked = not properly thought out/stupid
'That was a half-baked suggestion of Harry's.' 'Well he's pretty half-baked himself.'

cook

1. cook up = prepare scheme/story to deceive (also *see* **brew up,** Drink, p. 76)
'What new swindle's old Handley cooking up?'

2. cook the books = keep account books fraudulently

(n.) Too many cooks spoil the broth. Proverb = Too many people doing one job are bound to disagree over how to do it.
(The opposite is: Many hands make light work.)

eat

1. eat one's heart out = be very sad (grief-stricken) over s't

2. He ate his aunt out of house and home = He ate a great deal (generally used jokingly).

3. eat humble pie = back down and behave humbly
When the headmaster threatened to expel him for bullying, Lionel quickly ate humble pie.

4. eat into = use a great deal of (often money/supplies)
She ate into the money her uncle left her.
(sometimes used as 'eat a great hole in')

5. eat one's words = take back a claim/statement; say humbly one is/was wrong
He swore he'd never have an accident with the car but he had to eat his words.

flavour	I didn't like the flavour (attitude/tone) of/his remarks/ that article.
loaf	(n.) 1. Half a loaf is better than no bread.
	(n.) 2. Use your loaf = Think!/Use your brains (from Cockney rhyming 'loaf of bread' with 'head').
	(v.) loaf about = waste time I wish the staff would stop loafing (about) and get on with their work.
roast	to lie on the beach and roast (in the sun) (adj.) a roasting fire = a very warm fire
simmer	1. anger/annoyance which is barely or just under control Tom was simmering (with anger) at Brown's remark.
	2. simmer down = calm down He simmered down after awhile.
skin	1. remove the skin from a dead animal
	2. cheat/swindle s'o Three cardsharpers skinned him on the train.
	3. Keep your eyes skinned = Keep a sharp lookout/ Be alert.
stew	Let him/her stew in his/her own juice = He can stay in the trouble he's in as far as I care. It's trouble he made for himself.
taste	(n.) It (= attitude/behaviour/remark) left a bad taste in the mouth = It disgusted people/It was greatly disliked/It was considered most unpleasant (or distasteful).

Exercises

A. Which one of the four pairs (A, B, C, D) forms, or is part of, an idiom? Give the idiom.

1. A bacon	B eye	C biscuit	D ham
nose	apple	tooth	ear

2. A gooseberry	B jam	C mincemeat	D mushroom
give	sing	make	pick
3. A load	B work	C carrot	D job
pie	raspberry	task	plum
4. A loaf (v.)	B bake (v.)	C skin (v.)	D cook (v.)
out	in	down	up
5. A pancake	B juice	C bake	D cakes
mince	stew	butter	warm
6. A cucumber	B tart	C butter	D grapes
melon	gooseberry	bread	tree
7. A beans	B loaf	C stew	D cook
full	empty	cold	half
8. A beef	B tart	C pill	D mustard
tea	apple	sugar	vinegar
9. A baked	B roasted	C cooked	D stewed
half	all	fully	badly
10. A pickle	B skin	C poison	D words
jam	ear	meat	bite

B. Complete the sentences with an idiom and, as far as possible, rewrite in the passive.

1. The . . . that they held out to him to take the job was a very large salary.
2. At the gym you could always see boxers with their . . . ears.
3. A good many readers don't appreciate the . . . his remarks.
   The public doesn't always find them to . . . .
4. Someone had already put the information over . . . hours before the firm made it public.
5. What did they sugar . . . to get the men to work on Saturdays?
6. They were just about to . . . him with questions about his trip to New Zealand.
7. The niece had . . . a great deal of the money before the bank stopped her cheques.
8. The men said the new machines would . . . mouths.
9. People said the twins were identical – as . . .
10. Mary Anderson always . . . her novels with excitement.

C. Complete correctly with one of the four choices.

1. He managed to save his . . .
   A beef   B biscuits   C cheese   D bacon
2. I'd love your job. It's very . . .
   A fruity   B plummy   C salty   D sugary
3. Pamela has a . . . in every pie.
   A foot   B leg   C thumb   D finger

4. Frank's in a bit of a . . . Can you help him?
   A cauliflower B raspberry C pickle D biscuit
5. Now the manager knows, the . . . 's really in the fire.
   A fat B jam C cutter D loaf
6. . . . fingers! Can't you catch anything?
   A fat B jam C butter D ham
7. Don't make a . . . out of it. I only want to know the time.
   A dinner B pie C stew D meal
8. Tom looks a bit . . . off today.
   A stewed B cheesed C jammed D pickled
9. That fellow gives me the . . . He looks so gloomy.
   A cake B apple C grapes D pip
10. Let Bill . . . down first, then ask him again.
    A simmer B roast C bake D cook

D. Write out correctly any sentences you think are incorrect.

1. It's as warm as a toast in here.
2. That was a baked idea of Charlie's.
3. You can't have cake and have eaten it.
4. Harry laid on the beach roasting.
5. Jack ate humble pie quickly enough when he had to.
6. Keep your eye skin! There may be trouble.
7. Freddie said he wouldn't work for Phillipson's, but he had to eat his words.
8. The critics made mince of Carwell's new book.
9. Wally's broke. He hasn't the bean.
10. They left everything in apple-pie condition.

Drink

bitter

(n.) bitter beer
A (glass/pint of) bitter. Two bitters/glasses of bitter.
But bitters, 'I'd like some bitters' or 'Put some bitters in it' = a bitter liquid for flavouring cocktails etc.
e.g. a gin and bitters
Notice also: mild (n.) = (n.) mild beer. 'A glass of mild.'
And: mild and bitter = (n.) mild and bitter beer mixed.
'A mild and bitter. Two mild and bitter(s)/Two milds and bitter.'

champagne

(n.) The air was like champagne = The air was very fresh and stimulating.

cocktail

(adj.) cocktail biscuit/snack = cheese/savoury biscuit or item eaten with a drink before a meal

grog

(n.) drink of spirits (often rum) and water

(adj.) groggy = feeling ill/unsteady on one's feet (deriving from the *word* grog, but not used in the sense 'because of grog').

milk

(n.) It's no use crying over spilt milk = It's no good regretting a loss/mistake about which nothing can be done.

(adj.) 1. milky = used to describe a cloudy/unclear liquid; *see* **cloudy,** The Weather, p. 80

(adj.) 2. the Milky Way = The Galaxy, or sky's star circle

(v.) get information/money from s'o/an organization dishonestly
Harrington had been milking the funds for four years before the firm found out.

rum	(adj.) odd/queer/strange (origin uncertain, but not thought to come from the spirit – worth knowing, even so) A rum joke/person. That was a rum thing to do/say.
tea	(n.) A storm in a teacup = a lot of excitement/fuss/trouble over s't trivial/unimportant The papers had a sensational story about a ghost frightening a village, but the whole thing was a storm in a teacup. A man in a sheet was having a joke.
water	(n.) 1. hold water (as an idea/a theory) = be reliable when tested Einstein's theory about space being curved holds water. (n.) 2. pour/throw cold water on s't (idea/plan) = belittle/discourage it Beatrice wanted to study medicine but her family poured cold water on the idea. (n.) 3. be in/get into/hot water = be in/get into/trouble (n.) 4. keep one's head above water = avoid/survive money problems (n.) 5. spend money like water = be extravagant (n.) 6. water-biscuit = plain, hard biscuit eaten with butter and/or cheese
wine	(n.) Good wine needs no bush = Something very good or worthwhile doesn't need any advertisement. (v.) wine and dine s'o/friends = give s'o a good/special meal (at home or out)/entertain

---

Short questions

1. The air was like
   A grog   B brandy   C champagne   D rum
2. A storm in a teacup is something
   A serious   B unimportant   C imaginary   D to drink
3. An unclear liquid is
   A watery   B bitter   C milky   D groggy

F

4. What did Miriam get into for being late?
   A the soup   B warm wine   C hot water   D bitter beer
5. Explain 'a rum sort of person'.
6. What is the Galaxy's association with food?

Verbs, Other Forms and Details

alcoholic   (n.) an alcoholic = person who continually drinks more wine, spirits, etc. than his health can stand.

barrel   (n.) have s'o over a barrel = have s'o at a disadvantage
                      The bank has refused Robinson a loan. Now his creditors have really got him over a barrel.

boil   1. Rudeness always makes his blood boil (i.e. makes him very angry).

                      2. What it boils down to is . . . = What it amounts/comes to is . . .

                      3. boil s't down = condense/shorten s't (article/statement/story etc.)

                      4. boil (over) with indignation/rage

                      (adj.) The weather's been simply boiling recently = very hot
                      It's a boiling hot day.

bottle   1. bottle up = hold in/suppress an emotion (anger/fear)
                      The bus was very late but the passengers bottled up their annoyance.

                      2. where one army group bottles up another by cutting off the exit(s). Not the same as 'surround'.

bottleneck   (n.) where a road narrows, thus holding up traffic.

brew   1. What's brewing? = What's being planned/prepared?
                      Trouble's brewing (between them) = There's going to be trouble (between them).
                      There's a storm brewing (gathering).

                      2. brew up = cook up (q.v.)

corkscrew   move in spirals
The aeroplane corkscrewed to the ground.

distilled   (adj.) distilled wisdom = wisdom condensed/learned
over many years

dregs   (n.) The dregs (of humanity) = the worst kind of
people.
I'm afraid Alan's down among the dregs.

dribs and drabs   (n.) = in annoyingly small instalments
They paid the bill in dribs and drabs.

drink   1. drink s't in = listen to and absorb eagerly
The children drank in every word the teacher told
them about the fight between the dragons.

2. drink oneself to death/into the grave (through
alcoholic drinks)

(n.) 1. too fond of drink – too fond of alcohol

(n.) 2. be the worse for drink = have too much
alcohol and so be out of control of oneself

(n.) 3. drive s'o to drink = cause s'o to take to drink
= cause s'o to drink too much alcohol habitually.

ferment   ferment trouble = cause/make trouble

(n.) in a ferment = in a state of disquiet/excitement
The city was in a ferment over the bomb scare
at the hotel.

gulp   *see* **swallow,** p. 78

pint   (n.) = a pint of beer in the context: 'I could do with
a pint.'

pour   1. pour in/out = arrive/leave in great quantities
Crowds poured in and out of the shops during the
sales.
Telegrams, letters and messages of
congratulation poured in.

2. rain heavily
It never rains but it pours = Troubles seldom come
singly.

(n.) downpour = heavy shower of rain
see **water,** p. 75

sour   make bitter by experience
              Life has soured him.

              (adj.) bad-tempered/bitter in comment
              sour comment/face/-looking

swallow   swallow hard = gulp = react to insult/shock/surprise
              by swallowing with difficulty

Exercises

A. Which one of the four choices (A, B, C, D) is used as, or in, an idiom meaning the following?

1. to suppress something
   A tea   B brew   C bottle   D corkscrew
2. to extract money dishonestly
   A milk   B wine   C beer   D water
3. the worst kind of people
   A barrel   B dribs and drabs   C ferment   D dregs
4. to find a shock difficult to take
   A boil   B swallow   C brew   D pour
5. What's done can't be undone
   A milk   B gin   C wine   D water
6. to feel unsteady
   A pouring   B soured   C rum   D groggy
7. to discourage
   A tea   B corkscrew   C wine   D water
8. 'I'd like some beer.'
   A cup   B foot   C gulp   D pint
9. proved reliable
   A hold   B swallow   C pour   D drink
10. a strange remark
    A wine   B whisky   C rum   D cocktail.

B. Write or say an idiom or idiomatic form associated with each of these.

1. spirals
2. a gathering storm
3. an unclear liquid
4. a sharp-tasting flavouring
5. surviving financial problems

6. condensing a statement
7. having too much alcohol
8. a lot of news arriving
9. being excited
10. being extravagant

C. Write down, or say, sentences using each of the following as, or in, an idiom.

1. in hot water   2. distilled   3. but it pours   4. sour   5. mild and bitter
6. over a barrel   7. drinking in   8. good wine   9. boiling   10. downpour

D. Complete each sentence with one of the four choices: above, to, in, on.

1. It was a storm . . . a teacup.
2. He kept his head . . . water.
3. His theory boils down . . . a personal opinion.
4. Don't throw cold water . . . all her ideas.
5. The town was . . . a ferment over the news.

E. Complete suitably with idioms that include a verb.

1. The passengers . . . their annoyance.
2. The audience . . . every word.
3. The editor . . . the article.
4. I wonder what new scheme he is . . .
5. Tanks had got the enemy's troops . . . in the dock area.

The Weather

climate (n.) climate of opinion = general opinion/attitude (about s't)
The climate of opinion in the nineteenth century was against gambling.

cloud (n.) 1. under a cloud = out of favour/distrusted
Roy's been under a cloud since he mislaid the firm's new designs.

(n.) 2. in the clouds = daydreaming/elsewhere in one's thoughts
'You're not listening to me!' 'Sorry, I was in the clouds.'

(n.) 3. have one's head in the clouds = be always in the clouds/seem uninterested in material things
I think Dan must be a poet. He's got his head in the clouds.

(v.) 1. His/Her face clouded = He/She looked worried.

(v.) 2. Her eyes clouded (= filled) with tears.

(v.) 3. Her mind (was) clouded = Her mind/reason was affected.

(adj.) cloudy = unclear (of liquids – *see* **milky,** Drink, p. 74)

cloudburst (n.) violent (sudden) rainstorms

fog (n.) in a (complete) fog (about/over s't) = confused/puzzled
(*see also* **haze,** p. 81)
The police are in a (complete) fog over the theft.

(adj.) I haven't the foggiest (idea/notion) = I don't know/understand.

I haven't the foggiest what Nancy was talking about.

(adj.) fogbound = isolated/restricted by fog

frost　　(n.) s't that proves a disappointment
The evening was an awful/a complete/frost. The other
people turned out to be very dull and snobbish.

(adj.) 1. frosted glass = opaque (non see-through)
glass

(adj.) 2. frost-bitten = attacked/injured by frost
(body/plants etc.)

frosty　　(adj.) unfriendly
frosty-faced; a frosty glance/look/reception/smile/
welcome

(n., adv. of this) frostiness, frostily.

see **icy** below

hail　　(n.) a hail of bullets = many bullets passing or falling
(*see* **rain,** p. 82)

haze　　(n.) in a haze = in a fog (q.v.)

(adj.) hazy = uncertain/vague
Eddie was very hazy about the times of the buses.

ice　　(n.) 1. break the ice = an attempt to make a first
meeting friendly
Mr Williams broke the ice the first day in class by
asking the students to introduce themselves to each
other.

(n.) 2. cut no ice = make little impression/have little
influence
He doesn't cut any ice here. No one's very impressed
by him so far.

(n.) 3. be/skate/tread on (very) thin ice = be in a
dangerous/delicate situation
The Government wants to increase the tax on cars,
but they're skating on very thin ice. The public might
not buy as many.

icy　　(adj.); icily (adv.); iciness (n.) = very frosty (q.v.)

iceberg	(n.) She's/a bit of /an iceberg = She's very cold (in attitude/manner). *see* **cold,** p. 85
lightning	(n.) in the simile: as quick as lightning
	(adj. of this) a lightning change/sale/strike = very quick/sudden
rain	(n.) 1. in the simile: as right as rain = well/in good order/all right Everything's as right as rain again now that Mary's heard from John.
	(n.) 2. a rain (= hail, q.v.) of bullets
	(adj.) (put s't by) for a rainy day = save money in case of need You'd better/keep that money of Uncle Herbert's/ put it by/for a rainy day.
	see **pour,** Drink, p. 77
snow	(v.) be snowed under with s't = have a lot to do/ receive a lot of I'm snowed under with requests/work/bills/inquiries/ invitations = also deluged with (q.v. below, verbs)
	(adj.) snowbound = isolated/restricted by snow
snowball	(v.) increase rapidly (e.g. a situation, or the sale of s't) What began as a quarrel between two men snowballed until the whole neighbourhood was bitter.

Short questions

1. Since she insulted the committee, Betty's been under
   A the frost   B a dog   C a cloud   D the ice
2. 'Are you O.K.?' 'I'm as . . . as rain.'
   A good   B right   C fine   D sound
3. Being hazy about something means being
   A vague   B clear   C cheeky   D lazy
4. Taking a risk =
   A running   B sliding   C jumping   D skating/on thin ice
5. Explain 'I'm snowed under with bills.'
6. Say or write a sentence using 'fog' in an idiom.

---

thunder

(n.) 1. He spoke in a voice like thunder = a loud, angry voice

(v.) 1. make a noise like thunder =
The motor-bikes thundered through the narrow streets.
The police thundered on the garage doors.

(v.) 2. speak loudly and angrily
He thundered at them to keep quiet.

(adj.) 1. thunderous = very loud
a thunderous roar/thunderous applause

(adj.) 2. thundering = violent/very angry
He was in a thundering temper.
He gave them a thundering good telling off.

(adj.) 3. thunderstruck = amazed

(n.) 2. steal s'o's thunder = get the admiration/ applause s'o else would have had, by attracting attention to oneself.
(*see* **wind** below)

(n.) 3. thunderbolt = s't that causes great surprise or a shock
The news came as a thunderbolt/It was a thunderbolt.

wind

(n.) 1. go/run like the wind = go/run very fast

(n.) 2. There's s't in the wind = S't is being got ready in secret.
'Will taxes go up again?' 'I think there's something in the wind.'

(n.) 3. get wind of s't = have likely information/hear a rumour about s't
'They may increase taxes again. I got wind of it through one of the department's clerks.'

(n.) 4. Bob's got the wind up (he's frightened). He won't go anywhere by bus in case there's a crash.

(adj. of this) windy. He's windy of going by bus.

(n.) 5. put the wind up s'o = frighten s'o

(n.) 6. I'll have to raise the wind = I'll have to get hold of some ready money.

(n.) 7. sail (rather/very) close/near to the wind = go

very near breaking the law or doing s't improper
'Thomson sails very close to the wind with some of his
business deals.' 'Much too close, if you ask me.'

(n.) 8. take the wind out of s'o's sails = do/say s't
before s'o else who is about to do/say it; also
disconcert by going one better
Betty was just going to tell them she'd passed
the exam when Bill announced his own success in it.
It took the wind right out of Betty's sails.
Also = Bill stole Betty's thunder (*see* **thunder,**
p. 83).

(n.) 9. windbag = pompous, lengthy talker who says
nothing of value.

(n.) 10. windfall = money that comes to one
unexpectedly
Janet had a windfall. An uncle left her £3,000.

Verbs and Other Forms

acclimatize oneself to	get used to conditions/an idea/a place They gradually acclimatized themselves/got acclimatized/to (living in) London.
blast	(at) full blast = busiest/fullest point/state The machines/students were working (at) full blast.
blow	1. blow over = die down (subside)/be forgotten (often with 'soon') The quarrel/scandal/storm soon blew over. 2. blow hot and cold = be inconsistent in attitude, and therefore unreliable/be fickle Arthur's always blowing hot and cold (towards us). We never know whether he likes us or can't stand the sight of us. (n.) blowout = a very large, satisfying meal.
calm	calm down = cool down (*q.v.*)
chill	(n.) He was chilled to the bone = He felt very cold.

chilly	(adj.) = frosty (*q.v.*)
cold	(adj.) 1. He/It left me cold = He/It didn't impress/move me (*see* **ice**, p. 81).
	(adj.) 2. be left out in the cold = be ignored Nobody was friendly to her. She was left out in the cold.
	(adj.) 3. a cold look/smile/welcome = an unfriendly l/s/w
	(adj.) 4. a cold person = an unemotional person
	(nn. of 3 & 4) coldness/a coldness of manner
	(adj.) 5. cold-blooded = without feeling/pity
	(adj.) 6. cold comfort = s't that gives very small consolation 'Smiths have gone broke but they're paying the shareholders two per cent in the pound.' 'That's cold comfort.'
	see **shoulder,** The Body, p. 41
cool	1. Their anger/romance cooled (= became cool/lessened)
	2. cool down = become less angry/excited = calm down 'Cool down, George! Peter wasn't trying to insult you.'
	3. 'Let him cool his heels for a bit (= let him wait). I'm busy just now.'
	(adj.) 1. be/keep cool (= be/stay unexcited); a calm/cool person = adj. cool-headed
	(adj.) 2. cool attitude/reception = unenthusiastic/uninterested attitude/reception
	(adj.) 3. cool/a cool customer = impudent (in behaviour)/an impudent person. One who shows 'cool cheek'. 'That was pretty cool. He'd only just been introduced and he wanted to borrow £50.' 'He's a cool customer, all right.' 'Cool cheek, I'd call it.'
deluge	deluged with = snowed under with (*q.v.*)

Short questions

1. A thunderbolt is a
   A newspaper   B bad temper   C surprise   D motor-bike
2. They went to a restaurant for a good
   A snowball   B blowout   C blow-in   D calm down
3. Bernard's got the wind up. He's
   A afraid   B delighted   C tired   D found the money
4. Isn't Mary lucky? She's had a
   A chill   B cold comfort   C windfall   D snowbound
5. 'A voice like thunder' means . . . ?

---

dry

Dry up! = Keep quiet!/Shut up!

(adj.) 1. in the simile: as dry as a bone (or bone-dry) = very dry

(adj.) 2. in the simile: as dry as dust = very boring
The lecture was as dry as dust.

(adj.) 3. dry (of humour) = s't humorous said seriously
Mackenzie's very dry. He's got a very dry sense of humour. Everything's said so seriously but it's usually very amusing.

freeze

freeze s'o out = 1. in business, force s'o out by competition

2. in human relationships, exclude by coldness (*see* **cold,** p. 85)
Air Tours froze Plane Tours out by cutting their fares twenty-five per cent. Now they've got nearly all the business.
The other girls were jealous of her so they froze her out.

3. I'm/We're (absolutely) frozen = am/are/feel very cold.

4. freeze wages, and (n.) a wage freeze = period in which a ban or stop is placed on wage increases; when wages are/have been frozen.

hot

(adj.) 1. make it hot for s'o = make trouble for s'o

They made it so hot for the new manager that he had to leave.

(adj.) 2. be in/get into hot water = be in disgrace

(adj.) 3. (talk a lot of) hot air = talk without substance, often excitedly or showing off
The papers have had some new scheme for London's traffic but it sounds like a lot of hot air to me.

(adj.) 4. hot-blooded = passionate

(adj.) 5. hot-headed = excitable/impetuous (be a hothead)

(adj.) 6. hot-tempered = having a quick/violent temper
see **blow,** p. 84; **cake,** Food, p. 65; **collar,** Clothes, p. 50

warm

1. warm up = become gradually enthusiastic in a situation
Leslie warmed up as the evening went on. In the end he was one of the livelier guests there.

2. warm to s'o = get to like s'o
They quickly warmed to Michael.

(adj.) 1. = affectionate/enthusiastic/keen/sympathetic
a warm friend/audience/supporter/welcome

(adj.) 2. warm-hearted = kind/sympathetic

(adv.) warmly

wet

(adj.) 1. be/get wet to the skin = be/get wet through (soaked)

(adj.) 2. He's/It's (idea/plan) a bit wet = useless.

(adj.) 3. You're all wet = You're completely wrong/not organized.

(n.) He's a (bit of a) wet = n. of adj. 2. above; also = He's (a bit) dreary.

Details

breeze

(v.) breeze in/out = arrive/go unexpectedly
Harry breezed in this morning after a year at sea.

(adj.) breezy = good-humoured/lively (person)

adv. = breezily

gust

(n.) sudden display of feeling
There was one of Harry's usual gusts of anger but he soon cooled down.

shower

(n.) 1. collection, as in: a shower of blows/bricks/insults/stones (all in the hostile sense)

(n.) 2. but also used as in: a shower of bills/books/blessings (in the sense of things arriving together)

(v. of 1 and 2 above) shower with

storm

(v.) 1. take by sudden, fierce attack
The soldiers stormed the gun positions.

(v.) 2. storm into a place = taking as above by entering
The soldiers stormed into the town.

(v.) 3. also = enter a place angrily
He stormed into the house looking for his daughter.

(v.) 4. show great anger
He was storming over the tax increases.
The two drivers stormed at each other.

(adj. of this) a stormy debate/evening/get-together/session, etc.

(n.) The lull before the storm = a period of calm, looked upon only as a temporary interval before more trouble
'Father's been very quiet recently.' 'Yes, it's only the lull before the storm, I'm afraid.'

weather

(v.) weather the storm = survive a crisis
Mary's parents had various domestic and financial problems last year but they weathered the storm all right.

(n.) be/feel under the weather = be/feel depressed/unwell
Ted's been under the weather with his bad leg.

(adj.) 1. Keep a/one's weather eye open = Keep your eyes skinned. (*see* **skin,** The Body, p. 42)

(adj.) 2. weather-beaten· = appearance of s'o/s't that is
/works in the open air; mostly used in the phrases:
weather-beaten appearance/face/look

whirlwind   (n.) 1. very active, lively (person)
Margaret's a whirlwind.

(n.) 2. the simile: Margaret's like a whirlwind.

Exercises

A. Complete correctly and follow the instructions.

1. A Chilled   B Cold   C Iced   D Frosted/to the bone means . . .
2. I haven't the . . . what she meant. Explain.
   A frostiest   B foggiest   C cloudiest   D haziest
3. A Clouding   B Breezing   C Snowballing   D Thundering
   is what happens when a situation grows quickly. Give
   an example.
4. A Hot-blooded   B Hot-headed   C Warm-hearted   D Hot-tempered
   describes a passionate person. Use the word as an example
   in a sentence.
5. A A whirlwind   B An iceberg   C A deluge   D A weather chart
   is the only word for Jane, she's so lively. Explain the con-
   nection.
6. A Breeze   B Deluge   C Storm   D Chill
   is what angry people do. Use the correct word in a
   verb form, in a sentence example.
7. Wage   A dry   B cool   C freeze   D chill. Which is it?
   Use the verb form in an example.
8. A All wet   B All dry   C All breeze   D All gust
   describes a lack of planning. Use the expression in a
   sentence.
9. A Cold and wet   B Hot and dry   C Hot and cold   D Wet and dry
   is how inconsistent people blow. Explain the idiom.
10. A Thunder   B Windbag   C Frosty   D Fogbound
    was how she described a very wordy politician. Why?

B. Write, or say, ten sentences using each of the numbered items in, or
   as, an idiom. Do not change the form of the words.

1. in a complete fog over   2. as a bone   3. to make it so hot   4. frosted
5. voice like   6. the wind up   7. blown over   8. were left out in
9. frozen out by   10. warmed to each

C. Complete the sentences by including the words in brackets.

1. A shower arrived by today (post, of, bills)
2. The climate is smoking (against, of, opinion)
3. That murder was awful (frost, an, play)
4. The make change in Scene 2. (lightning, a, actors)
5. He got of plans a friend (through, wind, their)
6. There was cold in (news, the, comfort)
7. Mike's been to the storm (weather, able, always)
8. She took out his sails (wind, of, the)
9. It took a cool down (him, to, while)
10. I can't work full the time (at, all, blast)

D. Complete idiomatically with the correct item (A, B, C, D).

1. She gave him a . . . look.
   A gusty B foggy C cloudy D frosty
2. The two men were . . . at each other.
   A winding B hailing C thundering D lightning
3. We were . . . with invitations.
   A snowed B deluged C frosted D rained
4. Jack was talking a (1) . . . of hot (2) . . .
   (1) A heap B lot C ton D mile
   (2) A air B gas C wind D breeze
5. You'd better keep a . . . eye open.
   A storm B cloud C weather D rain
6. Who do you think . . . in the other day?
   A chilled B aired C showered D breezed
7. Her face . . . as she thought of the future.
   A fogged B clouded C hazed D iced
8. Put the £100 by for a . . . day.
   A wet B damp C rainy D dull
9. I'm afraid your friend doesn't cut . . . here.
   A an ice B the ice C some ice D any ice
10. Martin was sailing rather close to the . . .
    A storm B rain C ice D wind

General Exercises on all Ten Sections

1 Which is the correct idiomatic completion, A, B, C, or D? Explain the idioms.
1. He's like a bear with
   A a plum job   B pink elephants   C a sore head   D bitters
2. Poor Edward is under
   A the prunes   B the daisies   C his ears   D the clouds
3. The professor made . . . of his theories.
   A sheep's eyes   B apron strings   C mincemeat   D grey beard
4. The word has many . . . of meaning.
   A oaks   B kittens   C belts   D shades
5. The bag-snatcher showed a clean pair of . . .
   A sheep   B trousers   C heels   D biscuits
6. Cheer up, Molly! It's no good crying over . . .
   A dead roses   B flogged horses   C rainy days   D spilt milk
7. The whole thing was just a storm in . . .
   A a teacup   B a nutshell   C an olive-branch   D a pigsty
8. During the argument Alan got rather hot under . . .
   A the harness   B the claw   C the collar   D the blue
9. Tom had quite a fall. He was all black and . . .
   A green   B purple   C orange   D blue
10. There isn't room to swing . . . in our flat.
    A grapes   B a cat   C a primrose   D a raindrop

2 Give sentences using each of the following in, or as, an idiom. Do not change the form or order of any of the words.
1. buttonholed the headmaster   2. primrose   3. yellow
4. has been bulldozed   5. near the knuckle   6. of salt   7. sapped
8. a rum   9. put the fox   10. weather the

3 Which one of the four items forms or helps to form an idiom with the word that follows? Give the idiom fully, and explain it.
1.	A wallflower	B bread	C thunder	D cake	/eat
2.	A by	B out	C on	D for	/pocket
3.	A snow	B button	C thorn	D broth	/side

4. A moon	B bull	C goat	D red	/horns
5. A green	B ice	C milk	D pocket	/eyed
6. A bush	B pie	C hail	D fist	/bullets
7. A elephant	B nut	C arm	D sock	/crack
8. A cow	B coat	C willow	D head	/tail
9. A Wooden	B White	C Milky	D Rosy	/Way
10. A apple	B leopard	C lily	D coat	/spots

4 Give one idiom from the subject in brackets for each of these:
1. unsteady (Drink) 2. intelligence (Colours) 3. exclude (The Weather)
4. narrow-minded (Wild Animals) 5. mistake (The Body)
6. punish (Trees) 7. liven up (Clothes) 8. health (Flowers)
9. short sleep (Domestic Animals) 10. escape (Food)

5 Complete each space with one of the following: (i) a; (ii) the;
(iii) N where no word is necessary; (iv) any suitable word.
1. John's always willing to put . . . hand in . . . pocket to help . . .
   friend.
2. Jane let . . . cat out of . . . bag over Bill's present.
3. He's just . : . wolf in . . . sheep's clothing.
4. Well that really takes . . . biscuit.
5. Charles will get into . . . hot water if he isn't careful.
6. George's . . . remark was only . . . red herring.
7. Eddie made . . . good fist of . . . job.
8. I wouldn't put . . . shirt on its being . . . fine today.
9. His speech left me . . . cold.
10. . . . rose without . . . thorn, they say.

6 Complete correctly with one of the four items.
1. The meeting ended when the directors (1) . . . everything (2) . . . up
   (1) A will get B did get C had got D get
   (2) A buttonholed B milked C blown D buttoned
2. They said Martin . . . in yesterday looking very well.
   A storms B breezed C has flown D hoof
3. Tell Peter . . . it short so we can leave.
   A he lops B hem C to cut D hedging
4. Brian now wishes he . . . last year.
   A would have stormed in B has hogged it
   C was elbowing off D had branched out
5. There was little chance that the job . . . all . . .
   A is . . . coats B had been . . . butter
   C would be . . . roses D will be . . . cocktails
6. The general . . . a cat and . . . game for some time now.
   A has been playing . . . mouse D would blackball . . . cage
   C is heading . . . sleeve B poured . . . cheese

92

7. During the attack the troops . . .
   A earmarked   B were bottled up   C were browned   D poured
8. The teacher . . . several students since last term.
   A freeze out   B peppered out   C had trotted out   D has weeded out
9. There's Larry over there. . . . someone.
   A He snarls at   B He buttonholes   C He's roaring at   D He handing
10. Unless Alex . . . there'll be trouble.
   A knuckles down   B bottled up   C had capped it   D will storm in

7 By matching each numbered item with a lettered item find the ten
   groups that form or help to form ten different idioms. Then use
   each idiom in a sentence.
1. under   2. in   3. down in   4. before   5. up   6. with   7. below
8. on   9. through   10. off
A soup   B spectacles   C hare   D belt   E mouth   F brain
G wrong tree   H nut   I weather   J cart

8 Which one of the four items is associated with the meaning of the
   idiom in the sentence?
1. Betty's laughing up her sleeve.
   A ill   B anger   C cough   D secret
2. Sidney is very hot-tempered.
   A kind   B quick   C fever   D fun
3. Jack's got a couple of black eyes.
   A tired   B old   C fight   D rifle
4. Barton's got a cool cheek.
   A rude   B brave   C healthy   D wealthy
5. William's a bit droopy.
   A alive   B stupid   C sad   D clever
6. She's very catty, isn't she?
   A kind   B quick   C unkind   D travel
7. Where have you put the dust jacket?
   A car   B table   C coat   D book
8. They had a whale of a time.
   A expensive   B awful   C good   D fishing
9. My grandfather likes to tell chestnuts.
   A sad   B amusing   C serious   D memories
10. Alice would never play gooseberry.
   A piano   B tennis   C cook   D two

9 Complete the sentences idiomatically.
1. Greg finally took the bull . . . and inquired about a new car.
2. Mike's story took the wind . . . Jim's . . . .
3. She wasn't a bit sorry at the news but she managed to weep . . . .
4. 'What a bitter woman Joyce is.' 'Yes, I'm afraid life has . . . her.'

5. We've still got several problems to solve. We're not out . . . yet.
6. Joe's as cool as . . . .
7. You're in the wrong. You haven't got . . . on.
8. I know Bill's work is excellent. Good wine . . . .
9. You're spending far too much. You must learn to cut your . . . cloth.
10. Ask Edna to dance or she'll begin to feel like . . . .

10 Phrasal verbs in idioms. Complete correctly with A, B, C or D.
1. 'Smarten yourself up, and put . . . some dog.'
   A out   B off   C up   D on
2. Harry gave George a leg . . .
   A out   B down   C up   D on
3. As one scene faded (1) . . . , the next one faded (2) . . . .
   (1) A out   B on   C down   D off   (2) A for   B in   C over   D by
4. The detectives ferreted . . . the truth about the robbery.
   A over   B out   C at   D up
5. Their quarrel soon . . .   .
   A ran in   B dropped down   C blew over   D fell out
6. He buttered her . . . with all kinds of compliments.
   A on   B down   C over   D up
7. The staff were hedged . . . with petty restrictions.
   A over   B on   C in   D to
8. Walter suddenly blacked . . . when he was driving.
   A out   B off   C on   D in
9. What does his idea really boil . . .   . . . ?
   A up to   B in to   C down to   D away for
10. I don't think Mary's cut . . . to be a nurse.
   A up   B in   C on   D out

11 Find the numbered sentences which match the lettered ones.
1. The old man looked very weather-beaten.
2. It was very stimulating.
3. Edith apes her sisters in everything.
4. John was very angry.
5. Michael has a very good ear.
6. That's a rough fellow.
7. It made her gulp.
8. She said he was cowardly.
9. Arthur doesn't wear the trousers in that home.
10. It's reliable information.

a He sang the song after hearing it once.
b I had it straight from the horse's mouth.
c The air was like champagne.
d 'You're so lily-livered it isn't true!'

e Jane swallowed hard at the news.
f He led an open-air life.
g The wife is the dominant partner.
h He was simmering most of the afternoon.
i The child copies them.
j James is a very hard nut.

12   Either choose A, B, C or D or arrange the words correctly.
1. has been she often under the weather (Not a question)
2. A Nearly let Bill/B Let Bill nearly/C Bill nearly let/
   D Bill let nearly/the cat out of the bag.
3. Seldom (first word) it has taken so long to break the back of a job.
4. A Even didn't answer that cheeky cub
   B Didn't even answer that cheeky cub
   C That cheeky cub didn't even answer
   D Even that cheeky cub didn't answer
5. Greatly to give has he wanted Edwards the boot (Not a question)
6. A I would not do sooner/B Not sooner I would do/
   C I would sooner not do/D Sooner I would not do/
   something so hare-brained.
7. I knew that too well only Robert had been blackballed.
8. A They immediately found the pearl/B Immediately they found the
   pearl/C Immediately the pearl they found/D They found
   immediately the pearl/they knew it had been planted.
9. Never (first word) I a harder nut to crack have had.
10. A He drank almost himself/B He almost drank himself/
    C He himself drank almost/D Himself he almost drank/to death

13   Answer the following.
1. What can't a leopard change?
2. What is it no use crying over? Why?
3. What doesn't Basil cut here? Why?
4. What sort of life does that very quarrelsome family lead?
5. What is Billy still tied to?
6. Where is the fat? What does this mean?
7. Where do you keep someone if you don't want to become too
   friendly with him?
8. What do you paint the town? Why?
9. What path do you follow? Why?
10. What do you beat about? What are you doing?

14   Which one of the four pairs (A, B, C, D) forms, or is part of, an
idiom? Give the idiom.
1. A belt   B jam   C head   D cloud
   trousers   butter   water   foot

2. A dog   B boot   C blue   D wind
    goat   water   sun   raise
3. A tongue   B hide   C sleeve   D lose
    cheek   bull   roar   bacon
4. A brain   B poke   C brown   D rose
    sleeve   pig   currant   garden
5. A white   B cold   C willow   D smoke
    flag   soup   branch   eyebrow
6. A hound   B orchestra   C shell   D cold
    sense   face   out   cheek
7. A tooth   B eat   C green   D June
    ear   house   glass   hare
8. A own   B milk   C purple   D nip
    foot   marmalade   sleeve   bud
9. A true   B olive   C rose   D lift
    yellow   oil   window   hair
10. A hide   B sleeves   C dribs   D red
    nail   roll   dregs   lie

15   Complete the sentences idiomatically.

1. The railway couldn't stop the loaders . . . goods from the firm where the strike was.
2. Alan was made . . . pie.
3. None of the townspeople had expected . . . down like that by typhoid.
4. Mary never minds . . . a . . . dog.
5. I dislike . . . words put into my . . . .
6. The teacher determined . . . out all the lazy ones. (Flower idiom)
7. It's no good . . . hot under the . . . .
8. The directors got everything . . . up in about a week. (Clothes)
9. She pretended . . . under with invitations.
10. He can't stand her . . . like water.

16   Which one of the four items is not used in an idiom meaning

1. depressed or tired. A weather   B pink   C droopy   D blue
2. anger (1).   A storm   B thunder   C stew   D simmer
3. being or keeping calm. A coat   B hair   C shirt   D cucumber
4. a term of reprimand or insult. A monkey   B cub   C mouse   D pig
5. health. A roses   B pink   C scratch   D leg
6. problem/trouble/difficulty. A red   B wood   C sleeve   D pickle
7. throwing things. A salt   B pepper   C hail   D rain
8. anger (2). A red   B rub   C bear   D cow
9. running or walking. A leg   B hoof   C heel   D shoe
10. to keep quiet. A dry   B belt   C boot   D sock

17 Which are used in which? Which

1. animal   in an idiom meaning 'not much room'
2. part of the body in an idiom meaning 'have too much of'
3. item of clothing in an idiom meaning 'to change sides'
4. colour   in an idiom meaning 'gardening skill'
5. animals   in an idiom meaning 'a paper-chase'
6. flower   in an idiom meaning 'fresh'
7. tree   in an idiom meaning 'an old joke'
8. foodstuff   in an idiom meaning 'escape'
9. drink   in an idiom meaning 'discouragement'
10. kind of weather in an idiom meaning 'speed'?

Give fully and explain the idioms.

18 Complete idiomatically with one of the four choices.

1. She put something away . . . a rainy day.
   A on B after C with D for
2. The bank have got Smith . . . a barrel.
   A in B over C under D on top of
3. You want jam . . . it.
   A with B for C on D over
4. He leafed . . . the 'phone book.
   A into B over C round D through
5. James planted the idea . . . Harry's mind.
   A in B into C on D to
6. Sidney's . . . a blue funk.
   A at B in C into D with
7. George went to the manager cap . . . hand.
   A at B on C in D under
8. You're putting the cart . . . the horse.
   A behind B under C on to D before
9. They didn't make any bones . . . it.
   A about B of C from D with
10. We had to draw . . . our horns.
    A back B off C in D on

19 Complete suitably.

1. If Alice weren't so catty, . . .
2. If James had been less hot-tempered, . . .
3. He'll take the bread out of your mouth if . . .
4. They would have lopped off his head if . . .
5. Frank will get into hot water unless . . .
6. Life would be a bed of roses if . . .
7. If Billy doesn't stop monkeying with my car . . .

8. They wouldn't take Hughes off the blacklist unless . . .
9. You won't lose face unless . . .
10. If I were in your shoes, . . .

20 Answer the following.

1. He barked at her. How did he speak?
2. She was rather shirty with him. What was her attitude?
3. She purred at his remarks. How did she behave?
4. He was hedging. How did he speak?
5. She went scarlet. What was her reaction?
6. They hissed him. What mood were they in?
7. She got very ratty with him. How did she speak?
8. He was simmering. Did he laugh? Why, or why not?
9. She checked him. How did she speak?
10. He capped her remark. How?

21 The last lap (look in the dictionary for this and for what follows). To whet your appetite for more idioms, a few that aren't in this book:

1. It's six of one and half a dozen of the other.
2. Her name is on the tip of my tongue.
3. He led her up the garden path.
4. He's being very off-hand today.
5. A fat lot you care about your uncle!
6. He's a man after my own heart.
7. That was rather a left-handed compliment.
8. The whole thing is in the air as yet.
9. Her remark nettled him badly.
10. We're up to our eyes in idioms.